Experiencing Christ's Love

The Bible Reading Fellowship
15 The Chambers, Vineyard
Abingdon OX14 3FE
brf.org.uk

The Bible Reading Fellowship (BRF) is a Registered Charity (233280)

ISBN 978 0 85746 517 7
First published 2017
10 9 8 7 6 5 4 3 2 1 0
All rights reserved

Acknowledgements
Unless otherwise stated, scripture quotations are taken from The New Revised
Standard Version of the Bible, Anglicised edition, copyright © 1989, 1995 by the
Division of Christian Education of the National Council of the Churches of Christ
in the United States of America. Used by permission. All rights reserved.

Scripture quotations from The Revised Standard Version of the Bible, copyright ©
1946, 1952, 1971 by the Division of Christian Education of the National Council of
the Churches of Christ in the United States of America. Used by permission. All rights
reserved.

Every effort has been made to trace and contact copyright owners for material used
in this resource. We apologise for any inadvertent omissions or errors, and would
ask those concerned to contact us so that full acknowledgement can be made in
the future.

A catalogue record for this book is available from the British Library

Printed and bound by CPI Group (UK) Ltd, Croydon CR0 4YY

Experiencing
Christ's Love

Establishing a life of worship, prayer, study, service and reflection

John Twisleton

Contents

Foreword

'Community life would be all right,' I said once to a guest staying at the Monastery, 'if you didn't have to live with all these other people.' She smiled, then looked puzzled and then realised it was a little joke, which, of course, it was—in a way.

Jesus commands us to love one another, which sounds odd, but those of us who live in a religious community understand it. We wouldn't survive unless love had an element of obedience in it. Jesus tells us to 'love one another as I have loved you. No one has greater love than this, to lay down one's life for ones friends' (John 15:12–13). This love for one another isn't an option that depends on how we feel or on natural affection. It is the fulfillment of a commandment of the Lord and, done willingly, extends the love that the Father and the Son share with one another into human life and thus into the life of the world.

In order to be obedient, we must listen. We must listen to God in prayer, in silence and in reading Scripture. We must listen as we broaden our understanding of our faith. We must listen as God speaks to us through the words of others, as we strive to love and serve them. When we live like this, the heart is purified and we see more clearly. We learn, not only about God, but also about ourselves and how we can become more effective servants of his will.

If we are to co-operate with God, we need some structure and discipline. In this book John Twisleton encourages us to shape our lives so that we become attentive to God's grace and ready to respond, not motivated by our own desires but motivated by faith, hope and love.

Father Colin, CSWG (Community of the Servants of the Will of God)

Introduction

The clue to effective living is to find the main things and keep the main things as the main things. For over 60 years I've been working at both finding and holding myself to those things. I still have work to do here, so accepting an invitation from The Bible Reading Fellowship to write a short book on Christian priorities seemed a task both fit for the times and suited to the renewal of my own spiritual discipline.

You'd have thought that, as a priest for most of my life, I'd have this sorted by now, but although theological expertise helps me speak and write about experiencing Christ's love, its outworking in real life is all the more challenging. I don't just mean the obvious challenge of watchfulness, so as to practise what I preach, but the danger of overfamiliarity with holy things. There are, in fact, no professional Christians, though some get paid for their work. We are all amateurs, hopefully in the sense of devotees rather than incompetents—'not that we are competent of ourselves to claim anything as coming from us; our competence is from God' (2 Corinthians 3:5). This God-given competence is at the heart of prioritising the main things in life, so that our application to our work keeps getting pushed downwards in a list of attention descending from God, marriage, family and friends, church, study and exercise, right down to recreation.

As I prayed for God-given competence to frame this book, the Lord drew me to an image of his hand reaching down to me, and my own hand grasping his, with its five digits expressing five loves commended in his own summary of the law in Matthew 22:37–39: '"You shall love the Lord your God with all your heart, and with all your soul, and with all your mind." This is the greatest and first commandment. And a second is like it: "You shall love your neighbour as yourself."' Worship and prayer are to be seen as the heart and soul of our love for God, Jesus implies; but without study, engaging the mind with divine teaching, that love will be ill formed; and without service, love of neighbour, reflection and loving care of self, our loving God is a delusion.

Those five commitments—worship, prayer, study, service, reflection—make for me a hand that can grasp the hand of God reaching down to us in Jesus Christ, raising us into his praise and service with all the saints, an image of the grace (or favour) of God towards us. They provide the chapter headings of this short book, written during my time as Rector of St Giles, Horsted Keynes in West Sussex. I served eight years in this beautiful country village, helping people experience Christ's love and seeing my own devotion rekindled through engagement with the villagers. In his classic novel *Diary of a Country Priest*, almost a century ago, Georges Bernanos wrote of a French curé's struggles to be faithful—a work made into a powerful film of the same name. The priest is short-lived and the film ends on his deathbed as he famously utters, 'All is grace.'

'All is grace', since God's love is overall and in all. This is the 'main thing'—though we need to grasp it, and need reminders like this book of how Christians through the ages have best done so. May God bless you in reading what's ahead and, through it, may he give you a hand up into more of his possibilities for yourself, those in your circle and a world that sorely needs awakening to his love.

1

First love: worship

'You shall love the Lord your God with all your heart.'

MATTHEW 22:37

I am intrigued by worship. It's been around since before the world was made and will continue after its predicted meltdown. There's something awesome about connecting the heart of the universe with the human heart and lifting hearts together towards what is ultimate. Worship is extravagant, lacks restraint and goes beyond reason, in the way that love is bound to do. As a boy I dreamed of myself as a conductor of worship, raising my hands to invite folk into singing the praises of God. I see my ordination as a priest as fulfilling that dream. If worship is priestly, bringing people to God and God to people, it's priestly for all participants, not just the conductor, like music sounding upwards and outwards from an orchestra.

I am intrigued by worship because in it we touch the face of God, and something of him rubs off on us. 'Look to him, and be radiant,' says Psalm 34:5. When I was a teenager I found a remarkable place where Sunday services were like heaven to me. It was something totally different. The priest seemed like a saint, and the unselfconscious ceremonial, music and preaching made heaven above real and brought radiance to faces around me. I sought and found a word in the dictionary that summed it up—'numinous', filled with a sense of the supernatural, something that, up to then, I had not seen exercised.[1]

Being so intrigued by worship, I'm writing this book partly as a call to recapture the sense of the supernatural that worship in the Western church seems to have lost. As someone drawn to God by the supernatural in worship, I can understand why church attendance is in decline when so much of what we call 'celebration' feels so earthbound. To me, God has a sameness to us, yes, but is also utterly different in his holiness. When I worship on Sunday, I say, 'Holy, holy, holy Lord, God of power and might' and expect to leave church different, because of the expectations of God, worship and the church that were raised in me all those years ago.

Suspicion of otherworldliness has grown on account of religious fanatics, unhinged through excessive irrationality, who see God as terrifyingly different, with the sameness to us, who bear his image, lost. Religion, like money, power or sex, is God-given but gets man-handled! The etymology of the word 'religion' is linked to the Latin *ligare*, meaning 'to bind'. I am unapologetically religious—regularly attending Sunday worship—because I want to keep rebinding myself to God and his people. So much of my life loosens me from what's ultimate, from the love of God. I need to continually bind myself back to God through the five loves that Jesus describes in his summary of religion: '"You shall love the Lord your God with all your *heart*, and with all your *soul*, and with all your *mind*." This is the greatest and first commandment. And a second is like it: "You shall love your *neighbour* as *yourself*"' (Matthew 22:37–39, emphasis mine).

Worship and prayer are the heart and soul of my love for God. However, Jesus implies that unless I engage my mind with his teaching, in study, that love will be ill-formed; and without service (love of neighbour) and reflection (loving care of self) my love for God is a delusion.

Those five commitments—worship, prayer, study, service, reflection—make for me a hand that can grasp the hand of God, which reaches down to me in Jesus Christ to raise me into his praise and service with all the saints.

Experiencing Christ's love

How do you see God? Maybe he's close to you as a new Christian, but the warmth of the first encounter is cooling. Or perhaps, like the mature Christians of Laodicea mentioned in Revelation 3:16, 'you are lukewarm, and neither cold nor hot'. Either way, you are seeking to find strategies to know the love of God for real, inasmuch as it depends on you. The good news that we will return to, again and again, is rooted in a vision of God who is 'always more ready to hear than we to pray and to give more than either we desire or deserve'.[2] That lovely phrase from the Collect is read as part of worship day by day for a week every summer. Like so many worship texts, it serves to remind us of truth.

Like the Collect, this book is a reminder of love, of being loved and loving, for which words matter less than attitudes and deeds. It is, at heart, a reminder to stick at loving God in the five aspects that Jesus Christ invites us to, knowing that 'we love because he first loved us' (1 John 4:19).

No one writes more eloquently about the love of God in Jesus Christ than the apostle Paul, whose writings are a substantial part of the New Testament. Even his words, with all their force, crack as they address the love of God shown to us in Jesus Christ. When, for example, Paul speaks to the Ephesians of 'knowing the love of Christ that surpasses knowledge' (3:19), what does he mean? There's real ambiguity about the phrase 'to know the love of Christ' and it's helpful for us to examine it.

Does Paul mean Christ's love for us, or the blessings that come to us when we love God in Christ? Or is he talking about the love that God has, in Christ, for all that is—the love that he draws us into?

These are three ways of interpreting the phrase 'to know the love of Christ' and they are all precious insights. To know that the Son of God loved us and gave himself for us is, as Paul suggests in Galatians 2:20, our greatest motivator. To love God in the face of Jesus Christ is a blessing, since our devotion to him is God's gift, surpassing earthly knowledge; and, as Jesus himself says in Matthew 5:6, we will be fully satisfied if we want most of all what God wants. To know the love of Christ, thirdly, is to sympathise with and enter into God's compassion towards all people and all things, shown in the perpetual gift of his Son Jesus Christ.

I don't know which of the three interpretations of 'knowing the love of Christ' is right—it's probably all three! We'll follow them chapter by chapter as variations on a theme: downward love for us from God, upward love from us to him, and outward love from God and believers to the world. Whatever Paul meant by 'knowing the love of Christ that surpasses knowledge', I want that love, from him, for him and with him; and I wish that were so for all of us and for the whole of creation.

Christianity starts with God's love for us in Christ, and our response follows—a disciplined response which bears fruit in bringing others to experience Christ's love. That response is corporate, a receiving and giving out, with all followers of Jesus in this world and the next. It is corporate because the many-sided love of God can only be grasped 'with all the saints' (Ephesians 3:18). This truth is captured eloquently by Baron Friedrich von Hügel when he writes of the Christian calling to become 'a great living cloth of gold with not only the woof going from God to man [sic] and from man to God, but also the warp going from man to man… and thus the primary and full Bride of Christ never is, nor can be, the individual man at prayer, but only this complete organism of all the faithful people throughout time and space'.[3]

Experiencing Christ's love is nothing that we can do alone, which is why Jesus Christ left us both a plural form of prayer ('Our Father') and a festive meal (the Eucharist) by which to recall him. 'The cup of blessing that we bless, is it not a sharing in the blood of Christ? The bread that we break, is it not a sharing in the body of Christ? Because there is one bread, we who are many are one body, for we all partake of the one bread' (1 Corinthians 10:16–17). Some movements within Christianity narrow membership down to those with an individual experience of

Christ, who sense that they 'know the Lord', are 'born again' or 'manifest the gifts of the Spirit', but again and again these movements get drawn back to a mainstream understanding of full membership defined as being a baptised partaker of Holy Communion. This definition doesn't contradict any such experience or understanding, laudable as it may be, but rests on Paul's inspired insight that 'because there is one bread, we who are many are one body, for we all partake of the one bread' (v. 17). In a profound sense it is the Eucharist that makes the church, as much as it is the church that makes the Eucharist. 'Very truly, I tell you, unless you eat the flesh of the Son of Man and drink his blood, you have no life in you. Those who eat my flesh and drink my blood have eternal life, and I will raise them up on the last day; for my flesh is true food and my blood is true drink. Those who eat my flesh and drink my blood abide in me, and I in them' (John 6:53–56).

When I go to church, I go to worship and engage with God in Christ, present in bread and wine, in preaching, prayer and fellowship. Sometimes the sermon's dull, the sacrament feels empty or the prayers sound flat. One way or another—and it's good that there are a number of ways—Christ makes his presence real to me. Sometimes it's in a conversation or kind action that I experience afterwards, involving a fellow Christian. This reminds me that my commitment to worship isn't just as an individual but as part of something much bigger, that 'great living cloth of gold' which is the church, the 'complete organism of all the faithful people throughout space and time'.

Self-deception

I like writing. It's part of my calling and keeps me at the computer. There's where deception begins, and it may be true for you. I mean that you deceive yourself into thinking that your life progresses best when you're working on your own. Of course, when I am writing on a computer I can be writing or responding to friends—as I hope I am beginning to do right now as I engage you with the experience of Christ's love. That love is something shared, as we have already heard, and so is life itself. There are times, though, when I begrudge being taken away from writing to respond to other demands upon me. I can't live fully without balancing my own passions with those of others, those who share their lives with me, and that includes my fellowship within the body of Christ.

One of the tasks I have in winter is preparing the fire. It's great that Anne and I can sit, on occasion, by a coal fire which has something of its own life to share with us. I remember my father, Greg, taking a shovel of burning coals from the living-room fire to light the lounge fire when visitors came. We saw the red burning coals spreading their flame into a small heap of new coals placed on top of them. Sometimes there weren't enough coals brought to achieve this transfer, or too many damp coals were placed on the living coals, so as to quench them.

I think that the way fires burn challenges a major spiritual deception, which is that we can live a healthy Christian life as long as we go to church on occasion. Just as burning coals cool when separated from one another, so Christians need one another, especially in communal worship, to keep being fired by the Holy Spirit.

We deceive ourselves into thinking that we can experience Christ's love anywhere, so we don't need to worry about gathering with others to celebrate it. When I meet believers who've not been to church for a long time, I find that their love for God has cooled: he has become at best desirable, but in practice inessential to their day-by-day living. They have become practical atheists. In this falling away, a part is played by their sharing of their lives with those who implicitly reject God in Christ. Inasmuch as we have choice about who we spend time with, unless we choose to spend some time at least in worship, prayer, study, service and reflection, fervour for God will burn down, like coals isolated from a fire.

In his blog, Canadian pastor Carey Nieuwhof lists ten reasons why people are attending church less regularly:

- Greater affluence. (This brings opportunities to follow many more weekend options.)

- A higher focus on children's activities. (A growing number of children play sports and a growing number of parents choose sports over church.)

- More travel. (When people are out of town, they tend not to be in church.)

- Blended and single-parent families. (In a shared custody family, perfect attendance for a child or teenager might be 26 Sundays a year.)

- Online options. (Online church is here to stay, so anyone who attends your church has free access to any online ministry of any church.)

- The cultural disappearance of guilt. (If you're relying on guilt as a motivator to get people to church, you need a new strategy.)

- Self-directed spirituality. (In an age when we have access to everything, more and more people are self-directing their spirituality, for better or for worse. This is a characteristic of the postmodern mind, with its declining trust of and reliance on institutions.)

- Failure to see a direct benefit. (People don't see the value in being at church week after week. That could be because there isn't much value in it or because there is value that they simply don't see.)

- Valuing attendance over engagement. (When someone merely *attends* church, the likelihood that they will attend regularly or engage with their faith decreases over time.)

- A massive culture shift. (Church leaders who fail to recognise this will not be able to change rapidly enough to respond to the shifts that are happening. Change is unkind to the unprepared, so prepare.)

This list is a challenge to everyone who wants to experience Christ's love—a challenge to search their souls and see beyond the cultural shifts we're all part of, to those shifts in allegiance that have an impact on our love for God. As Carey Nieuwhof notes in his blog post, 'At our church, I find our most engaged people—people who serve, give, invite and who are in a community group—are our most frequent attenders. More and more as a leader, I value engagement over attendance. Ironically, if you value attendance over engagement, you will see declining attendance.'[4]

We deceive ourselves if we think we can come close to God without an engagement with the institutional church founded by Jesus. It's hard to imagine that we can come close to God in Christ without engaging with the meaning and power of scripture and sacrament. We can't receive Communion away from his church. Although we can pray and read the Bible on our own, for that prayer to be fuelled and his word to come alive, we need the school of worship and preaching that his church provides, even if that provision needs developing to enable us to engage with it fully in this generation.

I agree with most of Nieuwhof's points, but I have reservations on the last one, which speaks of 'a massive culture shift'. People aren't shifting from the spiritual (more on that later) but many are finding solace in less self-critical religions than Christianity. The loss of Sunday as a special day in so many countries has been a great shift, often allied to work demands that invade the family weekend. I know couples who have so little time with their children that taking them to church (unless the whole family is very keen to go) is a major achievement, to be attained once or twice a year.

People, by default, are having to find a spiritual path away from corporate worship. In 'self-directed spirituality', returning to Nieuwhof, there's a danger of being deceived into a vision of God that's so similar to ourselves that our own faces look back from it more than 'the light of the knowledge of the glory of God in the face of Jesus Christ' (2 Corinthians 4:6). God becomes the genie in our lamp, though scripture describes him as 'a consuming fire' (Hebrews 12:29). That fire energises the church, melting and moulding its members into an effective agency working for the salvation of the world, which entails the loss of selfish agendas in the service of the whole counsel of God. To use another image of heat, we could see the Holy Spirit received through God's church as a heavenly microwave that reaches inside its members, so as to defrost our cold-heartedness and our associated failure to love God. 'A new heart I will give you, and a new spirit I will put within you; and I will remove from your body the heart of stone and give you a heart of flesh' (Ezekiel 36:26).

Another deception derives from the consumerism behind Nieuwhof's listing of 'Failure to see a direct benefit'. The plain sense of worship is 'acknowledgement of worth', so failing to find benefit in worship is, in a plain sense, contradictory, since we attend worship to honour God. The congregation that fuelled worship in me seemed caught up in something above and beyond them, in unselfconscious fashion. Although the service was an elaborate High Mass sung from the English (Anglican) Missal, there was, through preaching and pastoral care, a drawing out of the self towards sacrificial service of God. This made liturgical sentences like 'Here we offer and present unto thee, O Lord, ourselves, our souls and bodies, to be a reasonable, holy and lively sacrifice unto thee' ring true.[5]

Rule of worship

Ever since that awakening to the Godward movement of the heart in worship, I have taken myself to church with an intention of self-offering, even if the service has at times been something that apologises for, rather than asserts, the upward call of God. If I hadn't made a rule to keep Sunday special over the years by worshipping with fellow believers wherever I was, I would not have chosen some of the gatherings where I've ended up! Especially as a priest, it's hard not to be 'consumerist' about our choice of church. I admit this, despite the reminder I'm giving here of worship being counter to any selfish attitude as an offering of 'ourselves, our souls and bodies, to be a reasonable, holy and lively sacrifice', refreshing our service of God's kingdom as citizens not consumers.

No rule of Christian worship can exclude either Sunday or the Eucharist, even if achieving both every week defies the pattern of life and work today and can be prevented by the unavailability of priests. If worship is a response to what God has done for us, on the first day of the week it recalls creation, resurrection and the coming of the Spirit.

This day, at thy creating Word
first o'er the earth the light was poured;
O Lord, this day upon us shine,
and fill our souls with light divine.

This day the Lord, for sinners slain,
in might victorious rose again;
O Jesu, may we raisèd be
from death of sin to life in thee.

This day the Holy Spirit came
with fiery tongues of cloven flame;
O Spirit, fill our hearts this day
with grace to hear and grace to pray.

O Day of light, and life, and grace,
from earthly toil a resting place!
The hallowed hours, best gift of love,
give we again to God above!
'This day at thy creating Word', William Walsham How

Bishop Walsham How's hymn captures the trinitarian motivation of Sunday worship. The 'hallowed hours' given back to God at the start of the week call into our souls the light that shone in creation (Genesis 1:1–5). On the anniversary day of Easter, we pray, 'O Jesu, may we raisèd be from death of sin to life in thee' (see Romans 6:11) and, on the memorial of Pentecost Sunday, that the 'Spirit, fill our hearts this day with grace to hear and grace to pray'. The obligation to worship on Sunday is a defining feature of Christianity, ever since the first Jewish believers changed their holy day from Saturday to Sunday— one evidence of the extraordinary event of Christ's resurrection. By attending Sunday worship, we underline, to ourselves and to the world around us, the historical events that are the basis of our faith. 'I handed on to you as of first importance what I in turn had received: that Christ died for our sins in accordance with the scriptures, and that he was buried, and that he was raised on the third day in accordance with the scriptures' (1 Corinthians 15:3–4).

It is very significant that Paul's underlining of Christ's resurrection on Sunday is matched by another emphasis, just as strong, on the necessity of the Eucharist:

> I received from the Lord what I also handed on to you, that the Lord Jesus on the night when he was betrayed took a loaf of bread, and when he had given thanks, he broke it and said, 'This is my body that is for you. Do this in remembrance of me.' In the same way he took the cup also, after supper, saying, 'This cup is the new covenant in my blood. Do this, as often as you drink it, in remembrance of me.' For as often as you eat this bread and drink the cup, you proclaim the Lord's death until he comes.
> 1 CORINTHIANS 11:23–26

As I have said in a previous book, *Meet Jesus*:

> The Lord's people gather on the Lord's day in the Lord's house around the Lord's table… The Sunday Eucharist is 'the hour of Jesus' in which we soak in his presence in word and sacrament, to be refreshed as his disciples.

Meeting Jesus in the Eucharist goes much further than the spiritual refuelling of believers, however. 'Proclaiming the Lord's death until he comes' has global and cosmic impact. The memorial sacrifice that is the Eucharist lifts participants into the worship that began with the angels before ever creation was, and will continue with the angels and 'the righteous made perfect' (Hebrews 12:23) into eternity. In what we could call 'the hour of Jesus', the Church's Eucharist, we see 'the lamb slain from the foundation of the world' (Revelation 13:8, KJV) and are lifted up into the consecration of all life to God's worship and service.[6]

I have found it helpful to keep such a cosmic picture before me as I gather, especially midweek, with two or three others around the altar (something well worth incorporating in a Christian rule of life, especially when shift work or family obligations override the Sunday obligation to worship). In such intimate fellowship there is a reminder that we receive the grace of Holy Communion in Christ's body and blood, both through bread and wine and through one another. Rowan Williams writes:

> One of the most transformingly surprising things about Holy Communion is that it obliges you to see the person next to you as *wanted by God*. God wants that person's company as well as mine. How much simpler if God only wanted *my* company and that of those *I* had decided to invite. But God does not play that particular game.[7]

Beyond a rule of attendance at your local church for the Eucharist on Sundays and holy days, I can commend engaging in bigger gatherings, such as cathedral-type choral evensong, Eastern Orthodox liturgies and non-liturgical charismatic-style worship. It's good to experience, on occasion, worship in a different Christian tradition. I find that such experience, once I get accustomed, can become a conduit through which God speaks to me powerfully, in the same manner that picking up and reading a new translation of scripture can refresh my engagement with the living word of God. Although my first numinous or supernatural experience was in an Anglo-Catholic church, I would count as highly significant in my life occasions when I have been present in charismatic churches, where the congregation has sung in tongues. This is a beautiful gathering of voices gently yet powerfully singing together, almost angelically, rising and falling in volume over several minutes, with great beauty and no human conductor. The silence that follows is to me as invested with God's presence as the silence after Communion at the Eucharist.

Following a rule of life doesn't guarantee an experience of Christ's love always in a tangible fashion, though all the evidence I see is that failure to worship moves us in the opposite direction, so that God becomes more notional than real. One of the monks of the Community of the Resurrection, where I trained as a priest, speaks of the eucharistic presence of Christ by using an analogy of love in the family: 'We may not always "feel" this presence. Just as in family life, it doesn't keep sweeping you off your feet with special experiences: it bears fruit over a long time. We gradually become steeped in the living story of Jesus, just as onions slowly become pickled.'[8] I like the pickled onion image of Christian formation!

Hand in hand

King George VI popularised 'God knows', a poem by academic Minnie Louise Haskins, in a Christmas message at the start of World War II. He quoted:

I said to the man who stood at the gate of the year: 'Give me a light that I may tread safely into the unknown.' And he replied, 'Go out into the darkness and put your hand into the Hand of God. That shall be to you better than light and safer than a known way.' So I went forth, and finding the Hand of God, trod gladly into the night.[9]

In this book I am presenting God's readiness to give us a hand up into his possibilities as we use five aspects of Christian devotion to hold to him, like the five interrelated digits of our hands. This image puts a key perspective on Christian devotion, namely that it can't save us; it just provides purchase for our Saviour as he grasps our lives to lead us forward. 'In this is love, not that we loved God but that he loved us and sent his Son to be the atoning sacrifice for our sins' (1 John 4:10). While we are incapable of glory unassisted, our salvation involves cooperation with God, whose word implies the same when we read, 'Work out your own salvation with fear and trembling; for it is God who is at work in you, enabling you both to will and to work for his good pleasure' (Philippians 2:12b–13).

In worship we experience Christ's loving uplift to the Father and get drawn into the ongoing momentum of his completed work, which impacts and is impacted by our prayer, study, service and reflection. For example, I recall occasions when a load of care deterred me from attending worship, but I followed my rule of life, attended, and was rewarded by losing that burden somewhere in the service, be it through sermon, prayers, Communion or a conversation afterwards. Something got shifted, and that shifting came from a reminder not to carry burdens that Christ has promised to carry, and a fresh realisation of what he has done for me and for all.

I can recall attending services which have so awed me that my prayer has flowed easily for days on end afterwards. In my experience the converse is also true—that prayerful preparation for worship builds an expectancy to encounter God in services. Worship is also helped by our study of scripture and of the world around us. Service is motivated by worship and inspires us in worship as we come before God with people's needs upon our hearts. In worship we also have time to reflect as the Holy Spirit is present in power to show us our needs.

Hand in hand with Christ we enter and leave worship, and we do so in concert with following the other four disciplines of prayer, study, service and reflection, which are all interconnected. These disciplines work together to make of our lives 'a living sacrifice, holy and acceptable to God, which is your spiritual worship' (Romans 12:1b).

Again, I quote from my previous book, *Meet Jesus*:

Our prayer should be that our worship pleases God before it pleases us. What we feel like during 'Jesus' hour' is, to a degree, immaterial compared with how our life-attitude of sacrificial service extends from that hour into the remaining hours of the week. It is arguable that the high point of worship is the moment when we leave the assembly—and the nature of our worship is shown in whether or not we leave more in step with Jesus, more ready to head wherever he wants us to go next.[10]

2

Second love: prayer

'You shall love the Lord your God…
with all your soul.'
MATTHEW 22:37

'Lord, thank you for the gift of this day and for your love. I give my life to you for the building up of the body of Christ and ask for your Holy Spirit.' I began today, as I begin every day, with that prayer and the sign of the cross—the so-called morning offering—as I got out of bed. A wordless signing with the cross, forehead to chest, left shoulder to right shoulder, is sometimes sufficient, as prayer is about both body and soul. 'I' is crossed out, with an aspiration that Jesus who died in my place might live increasingly in my place by his Spirit. Prayer is a lifting of the soul or inner being to God, inspired by God, part of the love offering that responds to the extravagance of his love more fully with worship, study, service and reflection. In prayer I am evidencing with Paul that 'I have been crucified with Christ; and it is no longer I who live, but Christ who lives in me. And the life I now live in the flesh I live by faith in the Son of God, who loved me and gave himself for me' (Galatians 2:19b–20).

Each day I have many people to think of, starting with Anne and the family, so it's natural to pray with her regularly as well as on my own. In prayer we affirm, moment by moment, what's real. My life and my thinking are influenced all the time by material concerns, which are natural to living with a body, but in prayer I open myself to the primacy of the spiritual. Like God's presence, prayer is invisible, an activity of the soul—although, like God, it can find a voice. Without that activity, life turns soulless, in the sense that it loses its place within the overarching compassion, truth and empowerment of the God who is ground of our being.

I remember once, as parish priest, attending a community meeting that many feared could turn ugly. After a few affirmative words to those attending, I said I agreed that we were in something of a hard place and in need of a miracle. I believed that good would come out of our meeting if we listened to one another and assumed the best of one another. I announced that I would spend the meeting quietly praying through the Psalms, with their different moods of joy and sorrow— which I did for almost three hours. One of the leaders said afterwards that he believed this action had turned the mood of the meeting. For myself, I felt my heart, carrying the people around me, caught up into and carried by the prayers that God himself provides for us in scripture through the book of Psalms.

When we can't find words to sustain the conversation with God that is prayer, God himself has words for us to use in the Bible, in his church's inspired liturgy and directly through the prayer-gift of the Holy Spirit.

When I pray for specific things, I am more surprised when no change occurs than when there is an obvious outcome, as at the village meeting. Prayer using the inspired word of God is indisputably powerful, which is why the church provides us with a cycle of praying through the Psalms, hour by hour and day by day. This morning I read a psalm and scripture as part of the divine office, which morning by morning includes the timely words of Zechariah's Benedictus: 'In the tender compassion of our God the dawn from on high shall break upon us, to shine on those who dwell in darkness and the shadow of death, and to guide our feet into the way of peace' (see Luke 1:78–79). As the dawn appears, I pray to be enfolded in the love that moves the sun above the horizon and yearns to shine in me and through me to serve those in darkness of spirit. Tonight, as darkness falls, I will make the prayer of the evening office my own, with Mary's Magnificat of thankfulness for mercies given to me and through me today. I will read aloud how 'the Mighty One has done great things for me, and holy is his name' (Luke 1:49).

Experiencing Christ's love

How do you pray *at all times*?

I believe that the church's mission is weak because its prayer is weak. When Christians hold themselves close to Christ, he is able to use them to release his possibilities into the world around them. When they fall away from intimacy with the Lord, they're useless as the instruments he has called them to be for building up his body in the work of the world's salvation. It's a costly distraction, which people have been addressing from the first days of Christianity, as in what's seen by scholars as the earliest document in the New Testament—Paul's first letter to the Thessalonians. It ends with this impassioned plea to early believers in Jesus Christ:

> Rejoice always, pray without ceasing, give thanks in all circumstances; for this is the will of God in Christ Jesus for you. Do not quench the Spirit. Do not despise the words of prophets, but test everything; hold fast to what is good; abstain from every form of evil. May the God of peace himself sanctify you entirely; and may your spirit and soul and body be kept sound and blameless at the coming of our Lord Jesus Christ. The one who calls you is faithful, and he will do this.
> 1 THESSALONIANS 5:16–24

This passage illustrates different aspects of prayer—praise, thanksgiving, petition and, by implication, the need to confess and loosen ourselves from our failings. It reminds us how God's sanctifying work in our lives is to be seen as the key dynamic and how, once he starts such a work, he always completes it. With that encouraging reminder, Paul bids us directly to look to the Holy Spirit, welcome words given from God, give thanks and rejoice in all circumstances and 'pray without ceasing'.

It's good to make a morning offering of our lives to God and to give thanks for graces given at the end of the day, but how on earth do you find a way in between to 'pray without ceasing'?

The idea of unceasing prayer sounds dangerous! Do you keep praying when you're driving or in charge of machinery? Isn't it good enough to make occasional aspirations to God to keep your life heading where you sense he wants it to go? Isn't it actually a lack of faith in God to pester him so, having entrusted your life to him? If prayer is a conversation with someone who's always with you, how on earth do you find the vocabulary?

Such questions came to me when God first began to challenge me by underlining this scripture passage to me. They are reasonable questions, but it's been my experience repeatedly that God has gently drawn me to go, out of love for him, into new territory that looks quite beyond what is reasonable. I recall times when I have felt an absence of God or 'quenching of the Spirit', being impelled to pray for the Spirit, and seeing how things happened to bring my prayer life back again in strength. On one occasion I asked for and received the gift of tongues, spoken of in the New Testament, which is a language of love beyond reason, voicing words of prayer to God effortlessly and in a strange language from deep in my soul. I think this gift came at a time when I had experienced a blessing after a time of aridity, was praising God a lot in my prayer conversation, but kept running out of words to express that love. The gift of tongues came after a priest told me that it wasn't something unhinged or irrational but a supernatural aid to personal prayer.

On another occasion I was suffering a sort of mental blockage to prayer that I might best describe as the equivalent of your body being besieged by mosquitoes! My mind had grown obsessively active with the coming and going of mainly useless thoughts, so I had increasing difficulty in settling it to pray. I needed a method to settle my mind into my heart, for it to be held into the prayer of my whole being. Once again, God worked to draw my attention, through holy people I knew, to the power of the repeated prayer, 'Lord Jesus Christ, Son of God, have mercy on me, a sinner.'

I've written elsewhere about the benefits of this so-called Jesus Prayer:

> 'Let the same mind be in you that was in Christ Jesus,' says Paul (Philippians 2:5). Invoking the name of Jesus places me in God's presence and opens my heart to his energy as I voice inside myself an ongoing desire to surrender myself to God's mercy. This is a very powerful dynamic, such that recalling the holy name of Jesus seems very often to bring God's power into play within my situation.
>
> The release of the mind into the heart is key to holy living, as it helps our thoughts and indeed our wills to submit to the work that God has for us and, through us, for a needy world. Repeating the Jesus Prayer is a means to this end, although it is a costly exercise because it involves continual use of the mind, which generates some natural resistance and sometimes a literal pain in the head. The internal flow of our thoughts is impossible to control fully but there are ways of disengaging ourselves and rising above that flow—and to this end the Jesus Prayer is a great servant.[11]

Experiencing Christ's love in prayer is always going to be a struggle, and it seems to me that God has planned it to be so, just as so much of life is, by his design, both a gift and a struggle. At the root of Christian prayer is the soul's eager longing for God, which great teachers on prayer, from Paul onward, see as being exercised continually, not sporadically and in a manner some way from how people are now tending to see prayer in a consumerist society. Although I readily testify to God in Christ as a God who has promised to answer prayer, my prayer is set within a personal relationship, within the fellowship of all the baptised, and is directed toward building up that body more than toward giving me what I want. Even the things that God knows I *need* can come very slowly indeed, and I have come to see this as being related to the greater and deeper picture of reality opened to us in Jesus Christ, which he is actively constructing through both our joys and our sorrows.

I pray to God as Christ-like. My prayer glimpses the face of Jesus Christ who illustrates the supremacy in the cosmos of what's personal. As such, my prayer, my life, is being purified of all that depersonalises and holds me and the cosmos back from being what God wants it to be. This makes it worthwhile to live in hope with unresolved tensions and questions, and not to let them deter my resolve to love the Lord with all my soul.

Self-deception

When people say they don't believe in God, I can sometimes conclude that I don't believe either—in the God they envisage. It's wonderful that there's a revelation of God rooted in historical fact and towering above any other alleged revelation in moral force. You couldn't worship a God who was less credible than the holiest mortal you know. Christianity is unique in showing a God who is credible in the face of suffering and death. Is there any depth of love or allied sorrow he expects of us that he hasn't felt first-hand?

Prayer as an awakening to God wakes us to reality. It's an ongoing purification of ourselves and our vision of God. What we see of God in prayer is dimmed by our sin, sickness and fear, so forgiveness and healing are eye-openers. This subjective side of prayer—knowing ourselves so as to better give ourselves—is complemented by the invitation to know God objectively as *God* really is, which we can know from scripture and creed. The way things are outside of ourselves, in the world, is also increasingly shown to us in depth as our faith and prayer deepen. We can then discern where God is working and in need of co-workers. C.S. Lewis writes:

The prayer preceding all prayers is 'May it be the real I who speaks. May it be the Real Thou that I speak to...' He must constantly work as the iconoclast. Every idea of him we form, he must in mercy shatter. The most blessed result of prayer would be to rise thinking 'But I never knew before. I never dreamed...'.[12]

Another deception we have to counter is the idea that prayer always makes us feel as if God is there. I remember visiting a brilliant novelist in hospital. He confided his atheism, which went with the assumption that those who believe always feel God's presence. I told him I'd read Mother Teresa's autobiography, in which she mentions that she hardly felt God's presence for most of her life. As I was mentioning Mother Teresa, a doctor walking by in the ward stopped abruptly and turned to us. Slowly he brought out a medallion hanging round his neck that had been given him by Mother Teresa when he trained in Calcutta. Both the atheist and I were pleased to touch that medal, and I felt God at work—ironic in a conversation where I had warned against relying on feeling!

God gives us enough experience of himself in prayer to keep us going. We read how Jesus started his ministry with an experience of the Holy Spirit at his baptism, and we then read of his being sent immediately into the desert to fast and take consolation in the word of God (Mark 1:10–13). Similarly, we find that times of blessing, when we feel God's closeness in our prayer, are followed by times of dryness, and it's those times when our love for God can really shine out. Pure love—God's love—is disinterested and doesn't seek any return, but mortal love for others is most often conditional on what we get back from them. We see pure love in the prayers of Jesus recorded in the garden of Gethsemane and on the cross, where statements of acute spiritual pain and loneliness are coupled with acts of faith—for example, when Jesus prays the opening words of Psalm 22, 'My God, my God, why have you forsaken me?'

If we see prayer as less than the commitment through thick and thin that it is, we are deceived as one making marriage vows would be if they thought they could say, 'All that I am I give to you' without consequences for their self-interest. To continue the marital analogy, keeping up our prayer life is a bit like parenting children. There are no short cuts, for the best always takes effort, even if God inspires and blesses the process, be it your prayer life, your marriage or your parenting. The way we use our time betrays our priorities in life, which for Christians major on three pursuits: the love of God, neighbour and self. This book is an attempt to detail how measured commitment to worship, prayer, study, service and reflection will guarantee that the main things in life stay the main things.

The other day, I was so busy that I cut my morning prayer. I'm sure the unsettling day that followed, which was quite chaotic, flowed from that absence and failure. I can't be too methodical in this analysis but I venture to suggest that my hour of prayer soaks up something of the eternal perspective of Christ's love. With that perspective reinforced day by day—and it needs to be day by day—I'm best equipped to make good decisions. Having exposed the centre of my being to Christ for a good time puts me in a better position to spot things I need to attend to here and now, as opposed to things that other people think I should be doing. Christian workers are sadly few, which is all the more reason for seeking the best use of our time and talents. We need to check this each day, and if we are to be in the best state of soul to judge, it all comes back to prayer.

When our prayer flags, it *can* be a 'dark night of the soul' experience, in which the purity of our love for God is being tested. But it can also be evidence of a gross failure in love for God, neighbour or self, of which we need to repent. The great value of having a spiritual director is that we find in them a mirror for the soul. Through regular conversations about our difficulties in prayer, we are helped to see and judge the difficulties, along with any issues we might need to address.

Jesus said, 'Whenever you stand praying, forgive, if you have anything against anyone' (Mark 11:25a). That teaching is reinforced in the prayer that Jesus gave us, which reads 'Forgive us our trespasses, as we forgive those who trespass against us'. Our prayer is hollow when we harbour sin or unforgiveness, and this can be a major self-deception. I can recall occasions when I've been troubled in spirit and have come to recognise that the troubling is due to a hurt I've received, often to my pride, which I need to forgive. Too often we are deceived into thinking that we need to put the one who's wronged us right, rather than accepting a humiliation sent to develop our humility and deepen our sense of need for God's mercy. This is a priceless gift which often arrives in unlikely and unpleasant wrapping paper!

Rule of prayer

The first rule of prayer is to pray as you can and not as you can't! In sharing on this subject, I hope to serve your exploration of a variety of lines, one or two of which might be suitable to build your intimacy with the Lord at this point in your life.

The second rule of prayer is to be honest before God. A lad found one of his dad's cigarettes and lit up. The experiment was going well until he saw his father coming, at which point he hid the cigarette behind his back and acted nonchalant. To distract Dad's attention, he started a conversation: 'Dad, can you help me with my maths homework tonight? I'd really appreciate it!' His father replied, 'Son, you've got to learn something—never ask your dad a favour when you're hiding a smouldering disobedience.' In the course of my life I've often asked for spiritual blessings from God and not received them, only to discover or be shown later that I needed to address an area of disobedience to him. Once it was addressed by repentance in that area of my life, I saw spiritual enthusiasm rising again, by his gift.

The third rule of prayer is to ask for grace for yourself as well as others. You can't get enthusiasm—literally a state of being 'in God'—without receiving from God, and you can't receive unless you ask. There is a scheme of prayer called Ignatian, after its compiler St Ignatius of Loyola (1491–1556), which is a helpful guide to use for imaginative praying from scripture. There are schemes available for eight-day or 30-day retreats.[13] I have been on three guided retreats following Ignatius' 'Spiritual Exercises' and recall being challenged by his direction, at the end of each of the daily meditations, to say a prayer of our own for a particular grace we have identified as needful for us at that time. Sometimes, when we pray, we get carried up to God in praise or towards the world with intercession, so that we neglect to seek our Lord's help for ourselves in the here and now. It's false humility to think that we are less important to God than any others we pray for, or that their needs are prior to our own.

The fourth rule of prayer is to pray with expectation. There was a recent attempt to release a film of the Archbishop of Canterbury and others reciting the Lord's Prayer, as a cinema advertisement—an attempt that backfired when the advert was banned. I was interested in the discussion generated, which included the perception by some that such a prayer couldn't possibly be seen as harmful. I found myself on the other side. To pray, 'Hallowed be *your* name; *your* kingdom come, *your* will be done…' is utterly counter-cultural, as it aspires to push aside so many other concerns that are enthroned around us. When we pray the Lord's Prayer, especially at the Eucharist, with arms outstretched in aspiration, we hold ourselves in expectation of seeing a work advancing until 'the kingdom of the world has become the kingdom of our Lord and of his Messiah, and he will reign for ever and ever' (Revelation 11:15b). Having such a prayer read in a cinema might well be disturbing!

The fifth rule is to have a set prayer time every day, as best you can. While I can experience the love of Christ always and everywhere, I know that I need to set a time and find a place for the Lord every day, *as best I can*. The last phrase is key. There are days when I'm on the move or have a continual string of responsibilities towards others, which mean that a formal prayer time is impossible. Suspending my rule of set prayer on occasion is like agreeing, when we've had a very late night, to turn off the alarm clock so that we compensate with more sleep in the morning. I'm none the less clear on my default position of giving the first hour of the day to God, something that's grown for me from ten minutes to half an hour to an hour over the course of my life. That hour includes slowly repeating the Jesus Prayer for half an hour, saying morning prayer from the Divine Office, with its daily scripture provision, and praying through various lists of people and intercession cycles.

The sixth rule of prayer is to adopt a means to pray informally, outside set prayer times. I mentioned earlier how God helped me to do this, at different seasons of my life, by praying in tongues and using the Jesus Prayer. There's value in short ejaculatory or 'arrow' prayers, like 'O God, make speed to save us', 'Jesus' or 'Glory'. The last word came to me from a friend called Ray Hubbard, a pioneer in the charismatic movement, who was much into saying 'Glory', attended 'glory meetings' and was a thorough inspiration to be with. He was large-hearted enough as a Baptist to see good in an Anglo-Catholic like me! I remember the privilege of blessing his body in its grave before his praise-filled memorial service, and how the sun shone over us, inviting a glory-filled prayer for Ray. I've inherited his tendency to say 'Glory' as a prayer word, alongside the longer Jesus Prayer.

The seventh rule of prayer is to talk about your prayer with others who are more experienced. Your life will then benefit from people like Ray and, in my case, Fr John Hooper. When I first met Fr Hooper I could sense something 'out of this world' about him, drawing me out of myself towards the God I sensed beyond him. Spiritual direction came, in my case initially by making a sacramental confession to Fr Hooper. Over the years, as I've moved around the world in my work, I've sought out prayerful folk from whom I can learn. I remember the forceful nun at St Beuno's in Wales who directed my eight-day retreat, who, recognising that I was a priest, expected me to pray for four hours a day and drop down to an hour on my return to my parish in Coventry. She was, nevertheless, a Godsend. It's my prayer that you might be inspired, through our brief spiritual companionship in this book, to seek someone at hand to be your ongoing companion. You'll best find that companion through praying for one, and also through engaging with your local church, whose priest or pastor will have folk to recommend to you.

The eighth rule of prayer is to listen to God. This is helped in my experience by reading scripture near to my prayer time. It has particular authority as the word of God, so it's an obvious place to go to experience Christ's love. Scripture shows us God in dialogue with humanity over thousands of years, so it's a great school of prayer. From there we can build a personal relationship with the God who has revealed himself and so become accessible to us in Jesus Christ by the Holy Spirit.

Scripture, summarised in the creed, also helps demolish our false images of God. Once I went on a retreat in a state of desperation. God seemed totally absent. My spiritual guide told me it wasn't that there was no God but that my vision of God had collapsed. He advised me to pray from scripture for a vision of God that was more to *his* dimensions and less to my own. I did. God answered. From that time I've made reading scripture and familiarising myself with its wisdom a key part of my rule of life.

The ninth rule of prayer is to be a theologian—someone who is interested in how God is seen, understood and loved by Christians across the world and down the ages. It was this that led me to the Jesus Prayer which has been such a help in sustaining my prayer over the last ten years. Seeing God in Christians led me to investigate how saints through the ages have formed their prayer. This golden thread of spiritual wisdom, reaching down the centuries, is evident in Eastern Orthodox writings, now made available in the West to great profit. As I wrote in the introduction to my earlier book, *Using the Jesus Prayer*:

> I have come to believe that there is nothing new in Christianity, just the need to enter the day-by-day newness of Jesus. In the following pages I look at how that newness has refreshed me through reciting 'Lord Jesus Christ, Son of God, have mercy on

me, a sinner' so as to realise in my life the biblical injunction to pray at all times. The Jesus Prayer is inhabited by Jesus, who is an effective reminder that God is love and has mercy on us frail mortals. It is a prayer discipline that states the simple good news of Christianity, provides Holy Spirit empowerment to bypass distracted minds, links worship with life, and resonates with the faith and prayer of the church through the ages.[14]

The tenth rule of prayer is to get praying *today*, without delay—maybe as an outcome of what you are reading in this book. Just as in any learning process, the bald truth is, 'I hear, I forget. I see, I remember. I do, I understand.' What matters is actually praying. With prayer there is never full understanding, and my ten rules should be seen in that light. They serve only to guide against useless action. I've listed some actions that will be useful as you attempt to find your own way, including being honest to God about yourself, admitting your need of grace, having expectations of God, setting a daily time, finding a way of praying through the day, seeking guidance, listening to God by reading the Bible and trying to be a theologian—knowing that we are *all* amateurs in that realm, even if we write books about God.

Hand in hand

Loving God with your heart and soul can be seen as being what worship and prayer are primarily about, linked to loving him with your mind in study, your neighbour in service and yourself through reflection. To repeat our central thesis, we have five basic Christian disciplines interrelated like the thumb and fingers of the human hand, set to grasp the hand of God reaching down to us in Jesus Christ.

Oh, that Christians were as mindful of their basic precepts as are Muslims, who also follow five precepts of faith, prayer, charity, fasting and pilgrimage. These five match most of what we are covering in this book, but I realise that I have written a chapter on prayer with no mention of fasting—which, in Christianity, is an aspect of prayer, like pilgrimage to holy places. I would commend my own practice of going without some food on Fridays and over Lent to commemorate Christ's love in dying for us, and fasting in tandem with prayer on occasions when there is an obvious need to pour our whole being into seeking God's will.

The *hamsa* hand symbol, seen across the Middle East, is understood in a variety of ways—as the hand of God warding off evil, a reminder of the five Muslim precepts or the five books in the Jewish Torah, or a general symbol of hope and peace. My interpretation of the 'five loves' invited by Jesus in Matthew 22:37–39 could be read into or out of the symbol as a simple reminder of balanced, effective discipleship. What's distinctive, though, about Christian as opposed to Muslim or Jewish precepts is the 'hand up' of grace that we might see in this symbol. Christianity doesn't see spiritual disciplines as attaining salvation so much as grasping the hand of the Saviour. Experiencing Christ's love in the five disciplines of worship, prayer, study, service and reflection means taking God's hand in ours, welcoming his loving provision of forgiveness and healing, which gives us a hand up into his possibilities.

> God, who is rich in mercy, out of the great love with which he loved us even when we were dead through our trespasses, made us alive together with Christ—by grace you have been saved—and raised us up with him and seated us with him in the heavenly places in Christ Jesus, so that in the ages to come he might show the immeasurable riches of his grace in kindness towards us in Christ Jesus. For by grace you have been saved through faith, and this is not your own doing; it is the gift of God—not the result of works, so that no one may boast. For we are what he has made us, created in Christ Jesus for good works, which God prepared beforehand to be our way of life.
> EPHESIANS 2:4–10

3

Third love: study

'You shall love the Lord your God... with all your mind.'

MATTHEW 22:37

I can't recall when I first gained my passion for study, but it was linked to Chemistry. I became fascinated with the make-up of the universe and literally pursued its elements. To my parents' disquiet, I produced chlorine in the shed and got obsessed with fellow halogen iodine and its explosive compounds. This line of study led eventually to a doctorate in physical chemistry and a research fellowship at Oxford.

Thinking about the elements and the way they connect up into compounds got my mind started on how the universe connects or should connect with God. It's natural for the human mind to leap between the two processes of identifying how and why things work, which operate in different planes. As a believer I have come to put mind before matter; I hold the materialistic worldview to be an insult to the human mind, which is so evidently able to transcend all things, being made in its Creator's image.

This capacity of the mind to study and go beyond our situation is a pointer to the unlimited mind of God. Such study is given new direction by the coming of Christ, as voiced in Philippians 2:5–6: 'Let the same mind be in you that was in Christ Jesus, who... was in the form of God.' Loving God with our mind goes far beyond academic study, into the study of a person, the one sent in great humility to make God known to mind and heart—Jesus Christ, true God and true man.

Studying Christ has been my lifelong learning. I was privileged to have a Christian education, which familiarised me with the Bible and the creed, the sacraments, commandments and prayer. These were parts of the jigsaw I had to assemble, once faith came alive and I discovered that 'in science we have been reading only the notes to a poem; in Christianity we find the poem itself'.[15] That poem contains my life, so that as a Christian student I crave formation more than information. My interest in the Bible is now complemented by an awareness of the interest that God in Christ has in me, which he expresses to me through the Bible.

To study as a Christian is a disciplined engagement of our whole being with the faith of the church through the ages, applying mind and heart to 'the whole counsel of God' (Acts 20:27, RSV) that we call catholic faith. That rich Christian term, 'catholic', speaks of whole, balanced faith as opposed to what is partial and sectarian. The Christian faith is something to grasp 'with all the saints'. Twenty centuries of scholarship and devotion serve entry into the unsearchable riches of Christ through prayer, Bible, creed, sacraments and commandments, instrumental in voicing his poem in holy lives.

It's a tragedy of our age to see naive religion, which comes about as people take the shortcut of a mind-bypass. Christianity isn't immune, for, if fervour of faith is vital, so also is the need to give reasoned answers for belief. This is clearly stated in the first letter of Peter, where we read, 'In your hearts sanctify Christ as Lord. Always be ready to make your defence to anyone who demands from you an account of the hope that is in you; yet do it with gentleness and reverence' (1 Peter 3:15–16).

No other religion so strongly holds to reason and faith, as inseparable wings lifting us to God, as Christianity. In the main blocks of the church, there is an openness to scrutiny of belief, unsurpassed by other faiths, though this has not always been so. Critical New Testament scholarship has continued now for two centuries and has done little to weaken its historical base in the resurrection of Jesus.

When we see Christian faith failing, it is as often due as much to failing catechesis (Greek for 'forming in teaching') as to failing evangelism, since enthusiasm for the gospel can sometimes be unthoughtful. While faith goes beyond reason (as, for example, in the resurrection), it doesn't go against reason: even the resurrection accounts can be examined and seen not as proofs but as pointers to the truth that is in Jesus (Ephesians 4:21).

Experiencing Christ's love

As a scientist I got excited, and still do, by new frontiers opening up before me as I applied thought to paradoxes like space being all curves in relativity theory and granular in quantum mechanics. I know that both theories work well independently but they can't both be right.[16] As a Christian I marvel at the ever-expanding vision of God before me, which contains paradoxes like God being three in one, divinity yoked to humanity, goodness permitting evil, free will linked to providence, and so on. No wonder Paul was led to exclaim:

O the depth of the riches and wisdom and knowledge of God! How unsearchable are his judgments and how inscrutable his ways! 'For who has known the mind of the Lord? Or who has been his counsellor?' 'Or who has given a gift to him, to receive a gift in return?' For from him and through him and to him are all things. To him be the glory for ever. Amen.
ROMANS 11:33–36

I remember this passage especially as it was set for evening prayer near the day of an accident that killed seven miners down Bentley pit in Doncaster, whose bodies I blessed in the makeshift mortuary, invoking the love of Christ over gutted wives and children. This was indeed knowing 'the love of Christ that surpasses knowledge' (Ephesians 3:19), for my study of the situation indeed tested my knowledge and my faith to the limit.

How could God's 'downward' love be evident in these premature deaths? Or how could 'upward' love be raised to him through our questionings? How could 'outward' love flow from God and believers to the hurting village? They did, by the grace of God, especially through one widow who became a shining light. Studying Christ in her made as much sense of the tragedy as anything else, so that, again with Paul, I was able to say then, and am able to say now, even in the face of the cruellest suffering, 'I want to know Christ and the power of his resurrection and the sharing of his sufferings by becoming like him in his death, if somehow I may attain the resurrection from the dead' (Philippians 3:10–11).

Loving the Lord your God with all your mind has to be something like that—linked to the sympathy for us expressed in Christ's suffering and the amazing incentive of his resurrection. Deep thinkers in every age have found their thoughts diffracted by the enormity of evil. The protest atheism of Albert Camus was built around this, as the great 20th-century writer saw a protest against life's meaninglessness as the only meaningful business. He was gently countered by Christian friends who affirmed the resurrection of the crucified Christ as stating God's credibility and sympathetic power in the face of evil.[17]

Such is basic Christian faith. It has a personal focus upon Jesus Christ as living Lord but it engages the mind through scripture, creed, sacraments, commandments and disciplines of prayer, which define the contours of Christian faith and church order. Application of the mind to Bible study, the creed, sacraments, commandments, and ways of prayer is essential Christian discipline. It's less a matter of informing us than of forming us as God's children, through 'taking every thought captive to obey Christ' (2 Corinthians 10:5).

If faith is the quality by which one believes, it is also the faith that is believed by Christians, the faith handed on to them by the community of faith, to be laid hold of intellectually as well as by heart and soul. God's revelation in the person and work of Jesus finds its simplest verbal expression in the biblically based summary known as the Apostles' Creed:

I believe in God, the Father almighty,
creator of heaven and earth.

I believe in Jesus Christ, his only Son, our Lord,
who was conceived by the Holy Spirit,
born of the Virgin Mary,
suffered under Pontius Pilate,
was crucified, died, and was buried;
he descended to the dead.
On the third day he rose again;
he ascended into heaven,
he is seated at the right hand of the Father,
and he will come to judge the living and the dead.

I believe in the Holy Spirit,
the holy catholic Church,
the communion of saints,
the forgiveness of sins,
the resurrection of the body,
and the life everlasting.
Amen.[18]

Although the first official mention of the Apostles' Creed is at the Council of Milan in AD390, scholars trace it back to an old Roman creed from the turn of the first century and to the three baptismal questions of the early church. Memorised then by the faithful, as it is today, hard copies were probably less at a premium in the early centuries, especially with persecution, which explains the lateness of its first documentation in the fourth century. The Apostles' Creed sets forth Christianity 'in sublime simplicity, in unsurpassable brevity, in beautiful order, and with liturgical solemnity'.[19]

Experiencing Christ's love is a matter of both mind and heart because God has made himself intelligible to us in Jesus, 'through whom he also created the worlds. He is the reflection of God's glory and the exact imprint of God's very being, and he sustains all things by his powerful word' (Hebrews 1:2–3). Our study of scripture and the world are linked on this account because God's word speaks through both the book of the Bible and the book of life. Preachers, on that account, prepare by studying both their set scriptural text and their people. It is an awesome truth that the Christ studied in scripture as the Word of God is also to be seen in the people and events that he sustains across the universe.

As I study the creed and discuss it with enquirers about Christianity, I find myself revisiting the imagery of a three-level universe, expanding on the linked miracles of the virginal conception and bodily resurrection—both mirroring creation out of nothing—how the doctrine of the church links both to the Holy Spirit and the communion of saints in heaven, and couching the hopeful ending of the creed in more contemporary language. This sort of study seems an essential duty, bound on all Christians so that the unsearchable riches of Christ may be accessed by the next generation without loss or distortion.

Self-deception

We had an invasion of molehills in the churchyard and someone suggested a novel way of getting rid of the moles: send for the bishop and confirm them! In my experience, people see confirmation as a one-off study, losing sight of the fact that it is an opening to lifelong study and learning, let alone worship. Being Christian is about recognising the mind that God has given us and applying it in an ongoing way to love him and make him loved.

We deceive ourselves if we think that study of the Bible, creed, sacraments, commandments and prayer is a one-off, though many people still pray as they were taught in childhood and haven't thought about the intellectual formulation of Christianity since their schooldays. Lifelong learning gets applauded in many spheres but not enough in the church.

What do we need to study? The faith of the church through the ages, which means gaining familiarity with scripture and the way Christians have formulated belief, ordered their community and defined their ethics, all with an eye to the study of the world around us. The balancing components are scripture, tradition and reason as a sort of three-legged stool, and different denominations give varying importance to each leg.

When Richard Dawkins published *The God Delusion*,[20] I was fascinated to see two reactions among fellow Christians. One was to read the book so as to engage with, or at least be familiar with, Dawkins' objections to faith; the other was to ignore it. Although I was in the first category, I grew in sympathy with the second, because we choose what we study, and to study something hostile to Christ can damage us. It's a point made by Paul when he writes, 'Whatever is true, whatever is honourable, whatever is just, whatever is pure, whatever is pleasing, whatever is commendable, if there is any excellence and if there is anything worthy of praise, think about these things' (Philippians 4:8).

If reason and faith both lift us to God, who is the God of both the Bible and the world, we should expect his truth to be available from both sources, so dialogue with people of other faiths or none shouldn't be alien to believers. Combative atheists like Dawkins aren't easily brought into dialogue, though some big Christian brains have taken him on directly. I found poignancy, myself, in the reminder at the end of his book that atheists are concerned above all to avoid 'self-delusion, wishful thinking, or the whingeing self-pity of those who feel that life owes them something'—fuelled as they are by a perception that this life is all that they have. *The God Delusion* challenges people of faith to get thinking, which is good. It inspires a degree of admiration for those, like Dawkins, who live energetically by their own steam without the Holy Spirit's back-up.

Dialogue is a great undeceiver. True conversation, flowing out of mutual respect, serves to clarify any misunderstanding of presuppositions. There is always a risk if our belief is ill-founded or unstable. The writer to the Hebrews shows wisdom on this when writing of 'the removal of what is shaken... so that what cannot be shaken may remain... since we are receiving a kingdom that cannot be shaken' (Hebrews 12:27–28). This mirrors Christ's promise to Peter in Matthew 16:18: 'You are Peter, and on this rock I will build my church, and the gates of Hades will not prevail against it.' Dialogue helps us find afresh the sure ground we stand on—which, for Christians, following Peter, is faith in Jesus Christ as the 'Son of the living God' (Matthew 16:16).

Socrates' ancient wisdom, 'The unexamined life is not worth living', applauds study. Only by regular study of ourselves can we identify causes for the ongoing repentance that helps keep us close to God. Spiritual progress involves tackling misinformation about God as well as self-deception. I recall being led, on a number of occasions, to get into my Bible and look at how God is seen there, to recognise how my own vision had shrunk and to seek in prayer a vision of God to fit more biblical dimensions. God is ever to be magnified and the discipline of study can be a magnifying glass.

I try never to allow myself to get deceived into defending God, the Bible or the church, for they are well able to defend themselves. Explaining doctrine is another matter. Contemporary media distort Christian truth so much that you can't avoid providing the occasional clarification to those who are finding obstacles to belief. One area of study that has been enormously fruitful for me is on forgiveness. There are occasions reported in the media when people really stand out for their forgiveness of others who have done them or their relatives enormous harm. When I study the media, these are the stories I keep in mind, so as to engage people better when they accuse Christianity of being guilt-inducing rather than guilt-ridding. Wherever society balks at passing over evil and engages with it creatively, we have a pointer to what God is ready to do for anyone who will bring him their hurt or sin for healing and forgiveness.

If one deception is in rationalising away the supernatural element of faith, evident in the forgiveness that brings resurrection to the soul, another deception is in defending elements of Christian tradition that are prescientific, as in the conservative evangelical opposition to evolutionary theory. In this realm I have been enormously helped by reading the priest-scientist Pierre Teilhard de Chardin (1881–1955), who prophesied the connecting up of human consciousness that we now experience in the global internet. His logical examination of the trajectory of evolution from inanimate matter to animation, then to human self-consciousness, extrapolates to the cosmos being made incandescent with the glow of a single thinking envelope.

This trajectory goes with Darwinian theory up to a point, then radically diverges towards the Christian vision, in which the God-given human capacity to converge and unify leaps beyond the materialist vision of 'survival of the fittest'. What is so powerful in this great thinker's work is his assumption of potential good in the scientific and technological advances of recent centuries, and his determination to see Christianity allied to this forward movement of the world. 'He utterly rejected the belief that the "schism" could ever be complete between the supernatural truth of salvation preserved by the Church, and the growing body of human truths that emerges from the work of mankind: "that can never happen".'[21]

In Teilhard's thinking, the meeting of minds, as through the internet, is the last stage before the uniting of holy hearts and souls in the communion of saints. In this process the exercise of human freedom, as in repentance and faith, is essential, since the spiritual momentum of Christianity, carrying beyond the physical and psychological to God in his holiness, respects the human option to choose God or not.

The option to love the Lord your God with all your mind goes with a determination to honour what other minds have made of God-given life, linking it with the forward vista opened up to faith through divine revelation. The fact that God has invested in our nature—physical, mental, spiritual, social—is the best evidence of its worth. Good things, like the power of thought as well as money, sex, power and so on, have a potential for good or ill depending upon the intention of human agency.

Christian faith, holding as it does that tomorrow also is God's, has a defiant hope about the future, on account of the life, death, resurrection and promised return of Jesus. Since God has invested in humankind, its good progress is a fruit of that investment in Jesus. This is a progress that rests incredibly on those of faith (who, in mind and heart, are determined to counter prophets of gloom, even those who are fellow believers), believing that 'the creation itself will be set free from its bondage to decay and will obtain the freedom of the glory of the children of God... All things work together for good for those who love God' (Romans 8:21, 28).

Rule of study

A rule of study looks to the three-legged stool of scripture, tradition and reason. We put scripture first, although a grasp of the interpretation of scripture (tradition) and a reasonable application of biblical principle to life are part of Christian lifelong learning and study.

> *Read your Bible. Pray every day. And you'll grow, grow, grow!*
> *Don't read your Bible. Forget to pray. And you'll shrink, shrink,*
> *shrink!*[22]

This Sunday school song, with its actions of growing up and shrinking down, captures it all. If we want to grow in Christ's love, we need to know that love, and we can't know it at all without knowing the record of it in the Bible, as the Bible itself reminds us. Here, for example, is counsel provided in the second letter of Paul to his protégé Timothy:

> As for you, continue in what you have learned and firmly believed, knowing from whom you learned it, and how from childhood you have known the sacred writings that are able to instruct you for

salvation through faith in Christ Jesus. All scripture is inspired by God and is useful for teaching, for reproof, for correction, and for training in righteousness, so that everyone who belongs to God may be proficient, equipped for every good work.

2 TIMOTHY 3:14–17

Scripture is the first object of study for Christians. We want to live in its world as much as we can. All our worship is scripture-based, carrying with it the invitation to 'read, mark, learn and inwardly digest'[23] section upon section of the Bible, which is often arranged to interpret itself in the lectionary. I am fresh from today's Passiontide Eucharist, where we heard Numbers 21:4–9 with John 8:21–30. We didn't need a preacher to work out that Moses' lifting up of a bronze serpent in the wilderness is linked to our Lord's prediction that he was to be lifted up on the cross. As people smitten by the serpent plague in the desert looked upon Moses' bronze serpent, they were healed. As people look to Jesus lifted up in word and sacrament, in our lives and the life of the church, they are drawn to the Saviour: 'I, when I am lifted up from the earth, will draw all people to myself' (John 12:32).

The more we familiarise ourselves with scripture, the more we catch on to such lines of coherence, which link to Jesus Christ, who is the clue to interpreting scripture.

Here are some questions I'm often asked about Bible study, and some of my answers.

- **Why should I pick up the Bible?** Because God is not just remote, above the clouds, but absolutely down to earth as the one who made us. He loves us so much that he wants to get into conversation with us and has given us his word in human words to engage with. If we pray for God's Spirit, he can make the words of scripture personal to us.

- **Where do I start?** Read one of the four Gospels in the New Testament, because you'll then capture how the coming of Jesus is prophesied in the Old Testament and makes sense of it. For a summary of the meaning of Jesus, try John 1:1–14 and 3:16; Acts 2:22–42; Romans 8; the letter to the Ephesians or Philippians 2:5–11. Many people find daily lectionaries, used in their church for morning and evening prayer and Eucharist, a good primer. They give a sense of others studying and praying with you. There are also lectionary resources, such as *Bible Alive*[24] and *Magnificat*,[25] to draw you along with their commentaries.

- **What about the Old Testament?** The Bible is a double-decker bus, helping us move forward with its two libraries of thought, brought together by the coming of Jesus. The 39 books of the Old Testament, plus the deuterocanonical writings (the Apocrypha), complement the 27 books of the New Testament. They contain the history of Israel, inspired poetry and ethical teaching such as the ten commandments (Exodus 20:2–17), to be read as from God in the light of Jesus Christ who fulfils the scripture (Matthew 5:17). This Christ-focus is made particularly clear when we read the second part of the prophet Isaiah. Chapters 40—66 contain the heart of the Old Testament and point forward in extraordinary fashion to Christ's coming and sacrificial death. Isaiah is the most-quoted Jewish source in the New Testament and reminds us of the cohesion of Old and New Testaments. His last section is full of encouragement for people suffering humiliation and exile, starting with words made famous through the music of Handel: 'Comfort, O comfort my people, says your God' (40:1).

- **What translation is best?** The New Revised Standard Version, New International Version, English Standard Version, Good News Bible and The Message (a paraphrase) are readily available, popular modern English versions that complement the Tudor English of the Authorised King James version of 1611.

- **What sort of Bible guides are available?** The Bible Reading Fellowship's *New Daylight* notes,[26] Scripture Union's online *WordLive*[27] and UCB's *Word for Today* online[28] are examples. Hearing sermons in church helps us to relate what God says in his word to our own context, as do Bible study groups.

- **What about studying Christian tradition?** With study, motivation is key, and it comes from your unfolding vision and experience of God. Tradition is essentially the reflection of Christians in past ages on divine truth, invoking Christ's promise, 'When the Spirit of truth comes, he will guide you into all the truth; for he will not speak on his own, but will speak whatever he hears, and he will declare to you the things that are to come' (John 16:13). We see the Holy Spirit bringing Christians to a common mind on doctrine and discipline through prayerful church councils, starting from the Acts of the Apostles (see, for example, Acts 15).

I recall how my first study of Eastern Orthodox Christian tradition came about. It followed a faith crisis, when I'd gone on retreat, having been advised to ask God to give me a vision of himself more to his dimensions and less in accordance with the narrow, dull image I then possessed. The answer to this prayer involved a sense of infilling by the Holy Spirit, which within weeks included the experience of praying in tongues. A friend who'd had this experience reassured me that I wasn't going mad and that if I read part of the *Philokalia* of Eastern Orthodoxy, I'd see that it was simply the prayer of the mind entering the heart.[29] I read this book, which later became a resource for discovering the Jesus Prayer. I also read a book by a Roman Catholic priest called Simon Tugwell, *Did You Receive the Spirit?* which provided similar assurance that Francis of Assisi and the Cure d'Ars, two of my saint heroes, let alone Pope John XXIII, evidently spoke in tongues.[30]

Through such study, I came to see tongues as a love language that is granted to the soul in answer to prayer, a gift that is subject to the will and (in Christianity at least) is not evidence of derangement or hysteria. Further study, using Kilian McDonnell and George Montague's *Christian Initiation and Baptism in the Holy Spirit*, helped me to see my experience of filling as a completion of infant baptism.[31] This insight has helped me invite others to seek the experience of baptism or filling in the Spirit as something optional yet vital, linked to the life and faith of the church, East and West, through the ages.

Twenty centuries of Christian worship, scripture study, devotion and moral reasoning are a terrific resource, made all the more available through the internet. Getting into the wisdom of the church through the ages helps to bring scripture alive and serves to bring us, and those who look to us as spiritual companions, closer to God. 'Will the Holy Spirit go with me if I enter a same-sex relationship?' 'Is my work on the stock market contrary to the law of love?' 'How far can we design our baby?' These are typical, difficult questions, which look all the more intractable without some grasp of Christian moral reasoning through the ages as a handle for decision-making. Sometimes we see the third leg of the three-legged stool—reason—as bringing things out of balance. Just because an action is possible, or a reasonable idea exists, it doesn't grant us full authority to proceed along that course or to follow thinking that has no guarantee of the Holy Spirit's ongoing accompaniment.

Ignatius Loyola (1491–1556) had a reckless youth, but reading the lives of the saints became, for him, a turning point. He could not dismiss the warm, joyous feelings they invoked in him, and this opened a door for the Holy Spirit to enter his heart. Studying the lives of the saints is a key to exciting holiness—written lives, but also the study of folk in our orbit who 'have something about them'.

Hand in hand

Experiencing Christ's love is our subject, in which I am presenting God's readiness to give us a hand up into his possibilities, as we hold ourselves to him with five aspects of Christian devotion like the five interrelated digits of our hands.

God's readiness to give us a hand to study him is rooted in Jesus Christ. Humankind's study of the book of nature through science evidences a questing intelligence that is a pale reflection of his, since Jesus Christ is 'the image of the invisible God, the firstborn of all creation; for in him all things in heaven and on earth were created, things visible and invisible, whether thrones or dominions or rulers or powers—all things have been created through him and for him. He himself is before all things, and in him all things hold together' (Colossians 1:15–17).

The love we offer God with our minds is a response to his own goodness, truth and beauty, with which we also engage in heart and soul and through love of neighbour and self. Many a time I find worship merely dutiful, but on occasion something touches me, lays hold of my imagination and takes me to scripture or to a spiritual writer with eagerness to build through study on that worship experience. Each day I read the Bible as part of set morning and evening prayer. Sometimes I can't remember what I've read, even quite soon after I've read it. Other times, when I've prayed a little more for the Holy Spirit to accompany my reading and prayer, verses light up as if highlighted on a computer screen.

Many Bibles lie unopened because their owners aren't praying and their desire to hear the word of God is absent. We all go through fallow periods, which is actually why holding a balanced rule of life is vital. A discipline of Bible study or reading the lives of the saints can trigger prayer, enrich worship, kindle service and aid self-knowledge. Conversely, a discipline of studying the news on a phone, TV or in print can kindle intercession or thanksgiving.

Might it be the case that God gave us sacrament as well as word so that we would still encounter him in material signs when preachers or Bible passages are dull? Worship, prayer, study, service and reflection are disciplines that hold a similar guarantee. Although two or three of them may fall away, we retain our grasp—or rather the Lord retains his grasp of us—through what is still directed to him. In the scheme of this book, study is the central discipline. Through it, worship is offered with fuller understanding, prayer kindled as God's word comes alive, service inspired by the observation of need, and self-knowledge deepened through the study we call conscience examination.

Study enlarges our horizon, raises our perspective and catalyses praise, as the psalmist observes:

When I look at your heavens, the work of your fingers,
the moon and the stars that you have established;
what are human beings that you are mindful of them,
mortals that you care for them?
Yet you have made them a little lower than God,
and crowned them with glory and honour…
O Lord, our Sovereign,
how majestic is your name in all the earth!
PSALM 8:3–5, 9

4

Fourth love: service

'You shall love your neighbour.'

MATTHEW 22:39

I've always been both an ideas man and a people person. When I went up to Oxford University, I quickly became involved in voluntary aid to pensioners. Sitting for an hour a week, listening to the fascinating stories of the elderly, was as energising to me as sitting in the college library, reading about polymers. Scientific research is engaging and mind-expanding but it's lonely. Your ideas get distilled by working in a group, but the narrow field you're exploring takes you away from common-or-garden life. One day, a colleague described the 'shallow conversations' he had overheard in a bus queue. It rang alarm bells. As a College Fellow, I was surrounded by brilliant, lovable yet eccentric individuals with an extraordinary focus. I needed a circle of acquaintance and of service that connected me with life lived by most people and the wisdom distilled from it that I found in abundance when visiting my pensioners. Some were evidently lonely, others more happy to be alone, but all those I met enjoyed connecting up with young people, listening and speaking.

Loving my neighbour is helped by my being generally interested in people. My danger is in getting so carried away with what I have to say (helpful, of course, when writing a book) that I fail to give space to affirm those I'm in company with, by the discipline of listening. A servant heart is one gifted with a bridle, able to curb its own need for attention so as to give sympathetic attention to others. How do we feel when we visit someone and never get a word in edgeways, or take part in a discussion where no space is given to hear what we have to say? In groups it's naturally difficult for everyone to be heard, but some of us are better at listening, taking things in and growing in wisdom through distilling the information that's offered by the more loquacious—of which I am usually one!

Experiencing Christ's love has downward (God to us), upward (us to God) and outward (God and us to the world) aspects. It's this last aspect that I find myself in when meeting a sister or brother who I know is also seen by God—and not just seen but *loved*, loved so much that God never wants to be separated from them. Like me, they are those for whom Christ shed his blood so that, though I might well be happy to manage without them, he never will. In serving others, that conviction grows in me day by day, but not without setbacks. I find it easier than our Lord to dismiss folk, especially when they seem to make my life a misery! Yet I know that Christ, the suffering servant, has mercy on me, looking upon me as much better than I am, and so I am fuelled by that knowledge to bear with others beyond what is natural to me.

A carpenter carves wood to make something beautiful. He or she also makes a mess, with wood turnings all over the floor. Sometimes I think of myself as wood being made good by Carpenter Jesus through the trials of life and the experiences that cross my self-interest. At other times I'm like one of those wood turnings, curled around a central emptiness, the emptiness of myself. To experience God's love, we turn *out*, not in. That's why the self-obsession and so-called narcissism of our age is such an enemy to our spiritual welfare. To spend so long on taking 'selfies' and posting 'status updates' about ourselves, rather than spending quality time with family and friends, isn't good for the soul. The self, like the eye, is given to look outward, not to look at itself, and so it makes no sense to itself. Human beings are made to devote themselves to something or someone outside themselves, even if our frailty is such that we continually console ourselves. Eating and drinking are natural. Jesus shows us the goodness that can flow from those appetites —for example, in giving us bread and wine as spiritual food. Yet the same appetites turned to self-indulgence can lead to destruction.

A young man I met last week told me he'd come close to death by indulging an appetite for drugs, and had prayed to God. Immediately he'd begun to see goodness and beauty in everything around him. This has set him at loggerheads with the negativity of his self-indulgent peers. God, in Christ, answered his prayer so that his thinking is now about what is good for him and for them. Human greatness lies in that very power of thought. Without it we'd be no better than other animals or inanimate matter. When we experience Jesus Christ, we are helped to rule our thinking by one who understands both its capacity and its frailty. This is a real turnaround, as the young man found, with the Lord turning us from self-absorption and indulgence towards God's praise and service of our neighbour. In thinking of ourselves less, though, as he discovered, we don't think less of ourselves. Rather, proud of our God-given dignity, we care all the more to counter threats to the dignity of others in a world that is far from what it was made to be.

Experiencing Christ's love

A Christian is someone who gives of themselves.

Christianity started in the self-giving of God as Christ was given to Mary, the 'servant of the Lord' (Luke 1:38) who went in haste to share news of Jesus with others. Her self-giving service is evident at Cana in Galilee, when the wine ran out at the wedding (John 2:1–11), and she kept faithful service to her Son right to the end (John 19:25–27). The clue to her service is the same as for any Christian—the loving empowerment of the Holy Spirit (Luke 1:35; Acts 1:14; 2:1–4). As we ponder Mary, we see healthy spirituality turned away from self to others. So much talk of spirituality today is about self-fulfilment. There's too little spirituality talk about how we can empower sacrificial service. Mary said, 'I am the Lord's servant' and, giving herself, was anointed by the Spirit to be a gift of love and prayer to the church through the ages. Her Magnificat song is an infectious song of service:

He has scattered the proud in the thoughts of their hearts.
He has brought down the powerful from their thrones,
and lifted up the lowly;
he has filled the hungry with good things,
and sent the rich away empty.
LUKE 1:51–53

Experiencing Christ's love is an entry into the flow of God's compassion for the world he made, fallen from him through human pride, now capable of being righted by the Saviour and his followers. Humility is the clue—knowing your need of God. 'Before destruction one's heart is haughty, but humility goes before honour' (Proverbs 18:12). Humility and love are inseparable, since the one recognises and inspires the other. How many times we get self-preoccupied in scenarios of obvious need, so concerned in honouring or contemplating ourselves that we miss the chance to serve, and the world moves on the poorer!

Richard Rohr distinguishes the servant (contemplative) mind from the (self-interested) calculating mind:

I distinguish the contemplative mind from the calculating mind. So, we who are educated, we who are Western, pragmatic, practical, problem-solving people—the mind that we think is the important mind is the calculating mind, which is constantly manoeuvring for self-interest. It's constantly manoeuvring for 'How can I look good, how can I be in control? How can I win? How can I make more money? How can I look like a better Christian than you?' This isn't love of God. This is all love of self. That's the calculating mind.

The contemplative mind is the mind that stops doing that. That stops using 'me' as the reference point. 'What do I like? What do I prefer? What do I need and what do I want?' That has to fall.

It doesn't fall easily and it never falls totally. First, you've got to recognise that that's where you operate from. It's a giant giving-up of control.

But, when you can accept the moment, the situation, the person in front of you without judgement, without categorisation… you live in the world with respect, with a kind of reverence. Not searching for superiority. Not searching for control, but letting things reveal themselves to you.[32]

There could be no better commentary on this teaching of Jesus Christ about who is to be judged favourably, which makes plain that contemplating and serving the needy is to be judged as service to God himself:

Then the king will say to those at his right hand, 'Come, you that are blessed by my Father, inherit the kingdom prepared for you from the foundation of the world; for I was hungry and you gave me food, I was thirsty and you gave me something to drink, I was a stranger and you welcomed me, I was naked and you gave me clothing, I was sick and you took care of me, I was in prison and you visited me.' Then the righteous will answer him, 'Lord, when was it that we saw you hungry and gave you food, or thirsty and gave you something to drink? And when was it that we saw you a stranger and welcomed you, or naked and gave you clothing? And when was it that we saw you sick or in prison and visited you?' And the king will answer them, 'Truly I tell you, just as you did it to one of the least of these who are members of my family, you did it to me.'

MATTHEW 25:34–40

Self-deception

I have a 'to do' list, and it includes visiting needy people in my acquaintance, being faithful to Matthew 25:34–40. It's a good idea in principle to marshal my time and energies for good and for God, but I wrestle with a number of deceptions.

Firstly, service isn't primarily something that can be organised quantitatively, since it is primarily qualitative. It's the work of the Lord, inseparable from the Lord of the work, which means making sure my heart is in it as best I can. If God lives in the present moment, I need to be there as well and not obsessed with some sort of care-provision target. The surprise of the righteous that they had directly served God in serving the sick hints at their self-forgetfulness, naturally pursuing good.

How do you best organise yourself for service? Recently I've taken to writing my 'to do' list on the right-hand side of a piece of paper, with a 'done' list on the left, to which I transfer items, crossing them out on the right-hand side. By having such a list, I'm helped to give thanks to God for occasional acts of service on my list with a reminder that 'I can do all things through him who strengthens me' (Philippians 4:13). Reminding myself of 'achievement' in this prayerful way helps me to see myself more fully as God's servant.

I deceive myself when I see service as a transaction I lead. It is far more complicated. The other day, I visited a woman in chronic pain whose husband was frustrated in all he did to help or care for her. As the two talked of their different hurts, I found myself lost for words and, finally, in tears. That God-given vulnerability placed me wordlessly alongside them and brought healing, something I could never have organised, let alone specified on a task list. If God, in Christ, is with us in serving others, he is also before us and to hand with his own resources, such as sending us the gift of tears. 'Likewise the Spirit helps us in our weakness; for we do not know how to pray as we ought, but that very Spirit intercedes with sighs too deep for words' (Romans 8:26).

Last week I was driving through the local town and got stuck behind a very slow vehicle. My impatience grew and grew until I had a chance to overtake the motorist, who proved to be someone I actually knew.

She saw both me and my evident impatience as I overtook her. There came into play a variety of emotions, including wounded pride! This led me to see afresh the importance of using things that counter myself as triggers for intercession. As Eric Milner-White puts it:

Pains… become pure grace of thy giving if offered up in prayer and shouldered to thy praise; scratches and troubles of an hour, no doubt, no more, yet stigmata, little stigmata, if brought to thee, the marks of the Lord Jesus on my being, wee supplements to one divine immeasurable pain, our mortal gift to an immortal love; and thus made healing for thy hand to use… Make clear both when and how I must take up the cross and follow thy wounded feet: for to enter the passion of my Lord and God is highest grace of all.[33]

We deceive ourselves if we think we can serve without the self-denial represented by the cross. Taking up the cross is a shouldering of little humiliations given us by life, so that they break the ego's shackle round us and help to incorporate us into God's own mercifulness as we pray for people, allied with our hour-by-hour frustrations. Intercession is a powerful outcome of frustration. Years back, I had a recurrent temptation that invaded my mind, and I resolved to counter it in this way. Every time the thought entered my mind, I turned it into prayer for the evangelisation of yet another province of China. I can't claim just for myself the remarkable spread of Christianity in China in recent years, but I know that my prayer played its part as a taking up of Christ's cross to counter my frailty and turn my heart outwards in venturesome love.

Through service to others, which includes intercession, we counter the ego which is our main deceiver. We also help 'the kingdom of the world… become the kingdom of our Lord and of his Messiah' (Revelation 11:15). That service is one of practical help to individuals and also one that addresses unjust structures. Yet another deception is to disdain socio-political involvement on account of its ambiguities. In many cases the most effective service comes through working beyond the service of individuals in need, to effect, with others, a God-inspired change to the organisation of society, so as to benefit everyone.

Loving our neighbour is about getting caught up in a transformational work in them, in us and around us. It's not straightforward, since people are so often contrary. Jesus observed this:

'To what then will I compare the people of this generation, and what are they like? They are like children sitting in the marketplace and calling to one another, "We played the flute for you, and you did not dance; we wailed, and you did not weep."… Nevertheless, wisdom is vindicated by all her children.'
LUKE 7:31–32, 35

We would be deceived to think that serving others in God's name goes without resistance and will be without trouble and discomfort.

Rule of service

Whereas rules of worship, prayer, study and reflection are relatively simple to organise, a rule of service is more complicated. I can make time to attend church on Sunday, pray daily, study and regularly examine myself, but making time to serve my neighbour is so open-ended as to be scary.

One overarching rule is to see everyone we meet as God's gift to us. That meeting, fleeting or ongoing, is given so that we see Christ before us. Monastic rules of hospitality spell out how visitors to the monastery are to be treated with all the reverence that Christ receives in worship, and it's good to emulate that ideal.

I find that my conversations with and about people, minutes after worship, can occasionally be quite out of order in their lack of consideration. This awakens me to a discipline of using words to God's praise and service with as loving an intention as I am able to give, whether I'm at praise or in service. At other times, commitment to worship and prayer seems like an excuse for shirking practical service, so that on occasion I've abandoned God's praise to serve him in my neighbour. Living to God's praise is hollow without consideration of the needy, and I need a regular reminder of this. A helpful aid is to pick up and read through the short yet powerful first letter of John. This letter beautifully weaves together the 'downward' love for us from God, 'upward' love from us to him, and 'outward' love from God and ourselves into service of our neighbour. 'Those who say, "I love God", and hate their brothers or sisters, are liars; for those who do not love a brother or sister whom they have seen, cannot love God whom they have not seen. The commandment we have from him is this: those who love God must love their brothers and sisters also' (1 John 4:20–21).

Most often I am reminded of my rule to serve others by lost opportunities. I look back on my day and see poor stewardship of my time, talents and money, given me by God for consecration to his praise and the service of my neighbour. Many church members are helped, by regular teaching on Christian stewardship, to reflect year by year on how they use their gifts and to prayerfully discern the optimum use of their time, talents and money. Most Christians serve within a body of local believers who, from time to time, organise community ministries. In my village church, members agreed to establish a monthly village lunch, which continues through a team of local chefs to provide a high-quality meal at a reasonable price, and it is very popular. Twenty people on a monthly chef rota lend their talents to serve this regular get-together of the community, which is a great servant of well-being.

In 2016, our Anglican bishop asked all parishes to join in with the Roman Catholic Year of Mercy proclaimed by Pope Francis, with a focus on renewing Christian service. I found it helpful to reflect on the so-called corporal and spiritual works of mercy owned by all Christians (minus the prayer for the departed in some quarters).

Here they are, listed in two groups of seven:

Corporal works of mercy

- Feed the hungry
- Give drink to the thirsty
- Clothe the naked
- Welcome the stranger
- Heal the sick
- Visit the imprisoned
- Bury the dead

Spiritual works of mercy

- Counsel the doubtful
- Instruct the ignorant
- Admonish sinners
- Comfort the afflicted
- Forgive offences
- Bear patiently those who do us ill
- Pray for the living and the dead[34]

Lists like these, drawn from scripture and the faith and practice of Christians down through the ages, are a valuable wake-up call for service in its many facets.

The corporal works of mercy focus on serving obvious physical needs and are drawn from Matthew 25, with the last work, 'bury the dead', picking up on teaching in the deuterocanonical book of Tobit. The spiritual works of mercy emphasise the service of faith, through counselling the doubtful, instructing the ignorant and admonishing sinners—when, of course, given opportunity to do so! Forgiving, bearing patiently and praying for others are services we must not undervalue, since remaining prayerful and peaceable means that our actions are invested with greater force.

Hand in hand

The idea of serving others through a monthly village lunch came out of a Lenten prayer and study group. Many ventures of service flow from worship, prayer, study and reflection. The upward, downward and outward flows of God's love in Christ go hand in hand. By faith we get caught up into that flow, with its two poles of praise and service.

The philosophy of the 'to do' list is about setting forth strategy for personal achievement, including service to others. For greatest effect, strategy needs to go alongside serendipity or surprises of the Holy Spirit. I am very used to strategic prayer as an accompaniment to liturgical prayer, the former being more oriented to specific needs, and the latter towards God and the universal call to creaturely dependence on him.

Organising worship and prayer linked to a mission strategy for church growth is helpful to servant ministry: churches need members to serve! Such a strategy makes me more aware of the loss of church members by natural means, such as when people move to better housing or residential care, and how the church needs to work hard simply to arrest membership decline. When setting sights for church growth, I am for ever impressed by the Holy Spirit's capacity to surprise, answering prayers in roundabout ways, disdainful of strategy. Last month, my 'to do' list included a lot of visiting of folk who were chronically sick and dying. I was surprised as I fulfilled those demands by yet another one, quite energising—to explain to someone at length about Christian faith. This explanation bore fruit in church attendance, and ideas and energies contributed towards a new venture of collaborative service in the community.

Strategy and serendipity hang together. We offer God our plans for service, individually and corporately, while humbly submitting to his will, which works out not quite as we imagined it. He sees the whole picture, after all, and there are many surprises for us up his sleeve. Hence the importance of prayer to the Holy Spirit, to be placed where

God wants us day by day. Such prayer has to go hand in hand with a readiness to see where God is working and moving us to serve alongside him.

In his Year of Mercy exhortation *The Joy of Love*, Pope Francis writes, 'I sincerely believe that Jesus wants a Church attentive to the goodness which the Holy Spirit sows in the midst of human weakness, a Mother who, while clearly expressing her objective teaching, "always does what good she can, even if in the process, her shoes get soiled by the mud of the street".'[35] This advice is set in a section of that exhortation entitled 'Accompanying, discerning and integrating weakness', which sets out mitigating factors in pastoral situations and 'the logic of pastoral mercy'. Reading this document reminded me how our service to others as Christians flows in love and never away from principle, as surely as the psalmist writes of love and truth walking together. The Christian desire to serve flows out of a loving heart and a conscience formed through love for the teaching of the church through the ages, with respect for those whose consciences have been formed differently.

Effective Christian service goes hand in hand with knowledge, gained through study of proven wisdom, and prayer to be used by God to free and save others, not least as they encounter, with and through us, his truth and mercy. Our ministry of service is kept on track by the discipline of regular self-examination, which recognises the positive as well as the negative side of our make-up. Recognition and corrected employment of our gifts in service is as important as owning up to our sins. Indeed, the parable of the talents makes clear that misuse of our talents is itself a sinful shortfall (Matthew 25:14–30).

I see myself simultaneously inhabiting three worlds under God: the mini-world of family, the midi-world of neighbourhood and the mega-world of mass media. The determination to be and to serve where God wants me to be and serve links to my familiarity with these three concentric worlds. Moving from space to time, the right apportioning of the time we give to attend to others in whichever of these spaces is key. Those nearest are, of course, dearest, so most of my time is spent alongside family, followed by engagements in the midi-world of community and church and the mega-world of social media, 24–7 world news and international agencies and instruments of service.

The prayerful and practical connecting up of these three worlds links to a gift of discernment about the best use of our time. When we sense ourselves to be in the right place at the right time, we feel a particular blessing upon our lives, which otherwise contain many missed opportunities. To be so discerning, connecting the people and worlds we inhabit, is a ministry of service in Jesus Christ, who works hand in hand with us to make God 'everything to everyone' (1 Corinthians 15:28 RSV).

To summarise on possible action points for service:

- Resolve to do the next thing in your life with all your heart.
- See everyone you meet as Christ before you.
- Read the first letter of John.
- Seek advice for the employment of gifts of service from your church.
- Look prayerfully through the corporal and spiritual works of mercy, listed above, and sense the Lord's invitation.
- Celebrate your service by instituting a 'done' list and praying through it with gratitude.
- Think through the balance of your engagement with social media and with people directly, as well as the balance between the mini, midi and mega worlds described above.

5

Fifth love: reflection

'You shall love… yourself.'

MATTHEW 22:39

I was in my late 30s, praying about marriage, when a letter came beckoning me to work in Guyana's interior, set for a single man. The letter lifted my sights to a new horizon away from home and away from preoccupation with my single state. After reflection, I identified God's call to essential work, training indigenous priests so as to make the sacraments available throughout Guyana's interior. I went, and as I went I met Anne, also heading for South America. She eventually joined me at the seminary, where we were married. It was a case of finding what was best for me in a roundabout way, linked to what God saw as best for others.

Regular self-examination, allied to visiting a spiritual director or soul friend, keep my life venturesome. I've missed many of God's invitations, for sure, but have spotted and followed enough of them to be convinced of the profound value of reflection. Some years back, the holy man who beckoned me to Guyana lay dying in a London hospital. I was one of the last to visit him and took my son with me, fruit of both my marriage and my obedience to his letter, which was a powerful reminder to the three of us of what it means to see where God is leading and to put your hand in his.

One of life's great challenges is to find God's future for yourself and venture towards it. All of us live with adjustment. Over the course of my life, I have adjusted to adolescence, manhood, marriage, parenthood, bereavement and many job changes. So much of life draws on our capacity to reflect, adjust and make sacrifice. In my adjustments I have found consolation in a God who has adjusted to humanity through the gift of Jesus, his suffering, resurrection and the gift of the Holy Spirit. My struggle with my single state occurred rather like Jacob's wrestling with God's visitor, described in Genesis 32:24–31, where Jacob says, 'I will not let you go, unless you bless me' (v. 26). My prayer and struggle about marriage came from basic self-love, but God heard that prayer, made me a missionary and yoked me to another missionary in his good providence.

In a park near where I live, there are many hollowed-out trees that are used as bat roosts. Storms 20 years ago destroyed much of the forest, and this destruction has been exploited. The same storms destroyed a farmer's house near me, so that the farmer, his wife and family had to move into an outhouse, suffering great and enduring loss. Thirty years on, the farmer's widow is a selfless Christian, with a radiance forged by suffering the tensions of imposed poverty. She has been hollowed out and filled with the Spirit. This woman has been able to live through suffering without bitterness.

We do not grow without pain, and a lot of pain is rooted in living with the tension associated with growth. Right love of self is established by God in us as we experience Christ's love in both sorrow and joy. My readiness to forgo marriage to serve the extension of God's kingdom was painful. In retrospect it was a bearing of the cross of Jesus, hollowing out my self-reliance through sorrowful months and years. Coming close to Jesus Christ, true God and true man, sanctifies human pain. It also opens up God's future for ourselves and for the world. The divinity of Christ, with the Holy Spirit, helps us enter a bigger scenario that shrinks our problems. The power of the cross to bring holiness out of painful adjustment is on show even in the church conflicts of our day. One priest, resistant to a fundamental change in the ordained ministry, describes the Lord leading him to praise God through tears for the joy that this change was bringing to many, while remaining opposed to it himself. Freed from the bitterness that abounded on both sides of the debate, he became a bridge-person across the divide who has brought healing.

'If anyone is in Christ, there is a new creation: everything old has passed away; see, everything has become new! All this is from God, who reconciled us to himself through Christ, and has given us the ministry of reconciliation' (2 Corinthians 5:17–18).

Experiencing Christ's love

Thomas Kelly's hymn, 'We sing the praise of him who died', describes the cross as 'the balm of life, the cure of woe' which 'sweetens ev'ry bitter cup'. Jesus uses his passion in every age to cleanse the wounds we carry as we live and grow and bear with suffering. A wound can fester or heal. In my teenage years I had the misfortune to experience an ancient medicine called a poultice. In this method, a hot covering is applied to a septic finger to draw out the badness. In my case, the poultice misfired. The wound festered under the poultice so that I lost the top of my little finger. When we draw the balm of the cross of Jesus down upon the wounds of our life, there is no festering of these wounds, but cleansing. The farmer's wife bore her storm damage, and the priest his church dispute, because they invited Jesus to cleanse the wounds they suffered. The Holy Spirit of Jesus was to make holy their pain and empower them to adjust nobly in their troubles.

The cross is God's adjustment. In the most profound way, God has said to us in Jesus Christ, 'I will adjust to you. I will change for you. I'll serve you—though it means a sacrifice for me.' Jesus suffered for us, showing God's adjustment to our nature, which brings it into his own extravagant love. Through the suffering and death of our Lord, we know that God expects nothing of us that he is not prepared to go through himself, and that through this sympathetic love he has opened for us the capacity to share the divine life (2 Peter 1:4b).

The story is told of a disaster that happened when two men were out skydiving. The apprentice skydiver's parachute failed. His selfless trainer managed to reach him across the sky. The two men descended at great velocity, suspended from the trainer's parachute. Seconds before they landed, the trainer adjusted his position to be underneath his apprentice and cushioned his impact at the cost of his own life. One man died in place of his colleague. He adjusted to take the full impact due to the other. In his crucifixion, God adjusted himself to bear the impact of the consequences of the sins of all people in every age: 'For lo, between our sins and their reward we set the passion of thy Son our Lord.'[36]

Experiencing the love of Christ is finding atonement, literally at-one-ment, with God. There are several theories of the atonement, none of which have been officially adopted by Christianity but all of which help us engage with its mysterious energy and sanctifying power. The skydiver story illustrates the so-called substitutional view, in which Jesus is seen to die in our place. In the sacrificial view of atonement, the blood of Christ fulfils ancient sacrificial rites by providing the sinless victim who alone can expiate sin: 'Christ loved us and gave himself up for us, a fragrant offering and sacrifice to God' (Ephesians 5:2). In the triumphant view of atonement, the thrall of evil powers over humankind are seen as being overcome through the suffering of Christ, who leads believers in his victory procession: 'Thanks be to God, who in Christ always leads us in triumphal procession' (2 Corinthians 2:14).

When a tree is felled, we see the beautiful rings within its trunk. By coming on earth to live and die, God shows us what he is made of and, through his rising again, invites us to be remade to enter his selflessness as we live through the joys and sorrows of life. Our experience of what God has done for us through the atonement grows when we reflect upon it and welcome its implications for our life, through the gift of the Holy Spirit. Christian belief in the crucifixion of Jesus links to the understanding of baptism as a sign that the 'old self was crucified with him' (Romans 6:6; see Galatians 2:19). Christian life is said to be 'ascetic', a discipline that is concerned with putting baptism into practice by putting the old sinful nature to death and opening the soul to new life in the Holy Spirit. It is this discipline that operates when we allow our sufferings to be made holy by Jesus who is 'the same yesterday and today and for ever' (Hebrews 13:8). The crucifixion of Jesus becomes a central part of our consciousness through our regular participation in the Eucharist, where we 'enter into the movement of Christ's self-offering'.[37]

When Jesus prophesied his crucifixion, he went on, 'If any want to become my followers, let them deny themselves and take up their cross and follow me. For those who want to save their life will lose it, and those who lose their life for my sake, and for the sake of the gospel, will save it' (Mark 8:34–35). When I look at a crucifix, I see the risen Lord behind it. I see myself and my frailty, yet I recognise how much I am loved in that frailty. I see God's invitation to move from self-knowledge and right self-love to the self-forgetfulness of Christ himself.

No one seeks the experience of pain but no one escapes it. Christian faith makes sense of it from the inside. This is the testimony of millions, and it is better lived than written about. To live without any ability to adjust to others or to God is a recipe for disaster. To live determined to see your circumstances as sent to bless you and hollow out your selfishness is to be taken out of yourself and raised to new life in the Holy Spirit. God in Jesus Christ adjusts to us, at cost to himself. The cross shows us the way to grow holy through the adjustments we suffer, and the Holy Spirit is sent to be our helper in this growth.

Self-deception

Here are ten deceits that deter reflection by undermining right love of self.

- **Thinking I don't matter.** A major deception in Christian life is to forget that God's 'downward' love is for everyone and everything, which includes ourselves. Our 'upward' love is raised to him, therefore, through love of both our neighbour and ourselves, and contributes to the 'outward' love flow from God to the world. There's a brand of 'unselfish' Christianity that goes over the top, in a self-forgetfulness near to self-devaluation. It can be harder for some of us to welcome love than to give it, so those occasions when we have opportunity to receive from others can be good teachers.

- **Never wasting time.** As a young man, Albert Einstein was told off for wasting time, although overall he made a wondrous application of his life to science.[38] Deep thinking, making friends and keeping them are among the fruits of keeping blank pages in the diary. One member of my family keeps two mobile phones, one for work and one for everything else, and the work phone is ignored at weekends. Phones with internet can keep us busy with our own and our work agendas, and we often need to decide between them—and we need to keep phone fasts when we really do waste time and make acquaintances wherever we are. Friends provide the nearest thing to holding a mirror up to our souls, but we cannot make friends, let alone witness to God's friendship, if every minute of the day is assigned a purpose.

- **Denying guilt.** Reading the newspapers and other media schools us in a culture of contempt for failure. We find ourselves fearful of taking responsibility for our shortcomings. We deny that the thing we have done wrong is blameworthy. It's not our fault, but is put down to anything or anyone else, our upbringing or just 'the way the world is'. The world is deceived in shunning the claim that 'all have sinned'; (Romans 3:23), but Christians believe it. We know that sinners sin and we know, most importantly, that God gives the assurance of forgiveness to those who face up to and admit their guilt.

- **Being shy of zeal.** A major deceit that stops us immersing ourselves deeper in the life of the Spirit is the fear of looking foolish before our friends, let alone looking zealous, with friendship-destroying zeal. We don't need to look far to see images of over-the-top religion in the media, or the failings of those who profess to be believers. We are deceived into preferring sympathy to enthusiasm, whereas the good news of Jesus needs both, in order to be spread. The gospel would never have reached us without believers who had overflowing faith, somewhere along the line. Thinking through how best to deal with stories of insensitive or arrogant Christians can help us forward here, and loosen us from the deception that living out what's true is always more important than 'speaking the truth in love' (Ephesians 4:15).

- **Avoiding contemplation.** Why do people keep so busy that they have no time to reflect? Often because they can't bear the pain of facing the truth about themselves, their situation or God. However hard the workplace, and however demanding are the many options we have nowadays for recreation, we are consigned to superficial living unless we take time 'to stand and stare'.[39] Contemplation is a counter to superficiality and brings us the chance of opening up to the God of life who wants us to share his life.

- **Going with the flow.** The herd instinct is absolutely natural to us, so we somehow get convinced that most people are on the right road and that challenging the thoughts of the majority is arrogance. This deception contributes to our social malaise. We try to conform Christ to people where they are. Whoever said people should be conformed to Christ?

- **Keeping control of your life.** The individualism of our age takes us off in pursuit of our own agenda, to the neglect of other people in our orbit. It's often a damaging way, as family and friends get left behind. If we avoid letting other people or external circumstances set our agenda, it fuels invulnerability and selfishness. 'It's your life and you only live it once' is a deception unless its truth is balanced by the sentiment, 'No one is an island'.

- **Deafening your ears to counsel.** Scripture speaks of a teachable ear (Isaiah 30:20–21; 50:4–5). We are led into deception if we are deaf to good counsel or keep ourselves absent from it through the choice of the company we keep. I remember heeding a plea relayed to me in the shape of Oliver Cromwell's words to the general assembly of the Church of Scotland: 'I beseech you in the bowels of Christ, think it possible you may be mistaken.'[40] Sometimes we need to give or receive counsel in as dramatic a form as this so that we are brought back to the way of Christ.

- **Living life strategically.** Most people don't plan to fail, they just fail to plan. It's good to plan our lives and be strategic, even about our prayers, but beware! Those who tell God their plans make him laugh, and we discover the truth of this again and again through his surprises. Our lives are filled with surprise—serendipity—more than worked-out strategy. Strategic thinking is good in itself but it can deceive us into thinking that we are in charge of our lives.

- **Disbelief in the devil.** The flipside to failing to see our importance to God is to fail to see the power of our adversary, the devil, even if he has only the power that we ourselves grant him. Putting it another way, we are caught up in a spiritual battle that is being fought in the universe. If we fail to see, for example, the power of lies to hide the truth, we can end up living a lie ourselves. I believe in the devil but I believe that his only power is the power I give to him when I deceive myself into wrong thinking that serves self-indulgence.

Rule of reflection

Christianity is a historical religion, so we can trace its origins in particular events and see how reflection on those events has served the faith of the church through the ages. There is also the so-called 'apostolic succession', which is a succession of leaders and teachers who have helped to hold the church to the faith first handed to the apostles. The Bible witnesses to this faith, and Bible reading is key to right reflection upon our lives. It can become, by his Spirit, God's gracious interrogation, as has been mentioned in the earlier chapter on prayer. With its particular authority as the word of God, a rule of reading the Bible is an obvious aid to fruitful reflection.

Parallel to the continuity of Bible and church teaching is a golden thread of spiritual direction, reaching down through the ages, by which the prayer of God's people has been secured from generation to generation. In the chapter on prayer, I mentioned the value of talking about your prayer with others who are more experienced. Just as we need others to bring us to Christ, we need others to keep us close to Christ—a process that can be both informal and structured into different forms of spiritual accompaniment. I have mentioned the Godsend of the nun who directed me, on retreat, to become more generous in prayer, suggesting that I keep to an hour a day as an ongoing rule of life. I now see this as an essential rule to aid in keeping me close to God. I always pay the price for skipping the rule!

How do you find a spiritual director? You need to be connected with the church, so talk to your pastor, who should be au fait with the local network. If not, ask him or her to make enquiries for you among other Christian ministers. Mostly, folk accredited as 'directors'—a rather forbidding title—work more as spiritual companions or soul friends. In my experience of a variety of directors, few match up to the nun in my story. I put her intervention down to God doing some crisis management on my soul! Spiritual directors themselves receive guidance from others and live under God's mercy. The Holy Spirit is the real spiritual director but often uses open, prayerful conversations between companions to make his ways clear for individuals. In my diocese, there is an officer who provides a couple of names to enquirers from churches, with an eye to their location. The idea is to have an initial meeting to see how things go, and to change if the pairing is not an easy match. As a spiritual director, I make myself available for an hour or two, three or four times a year, and people come and go.

I link receiving spiritual direction with an allied discipline of sacramental confession. I choose to go to a priest for confession six times a year, before major Christian feasts, and extend the meeting into a spiritual direction session on half of these occasions. Christians disagree about the ways we can receive God's forgiveness, but all agree that church members should be accountable both to God and to their church.

Some are happy to use the minister as an instrument of forgiveness, while others see this as introducing a go-between who could detract from Christ. However, 'If you forgive the sins of any, they are forgiven them,' Jesus said to the apostles (John 20:23). For 20 centuries this ministry of forgiveness, of freeing from sin, has continued in his church, particularly through the ordained ministry. Jesus died so that we might be forgiven, but we have to receive that forgiveness. 'Confess your sins to one another... so that you may be healed,' James says in his letter (5:16). We need healing from guilt, the feeling that our sins aren't forgiven. We also need our church membership to be renewed when we sin and let the side down.

The ministry of forgiveness can be unstructured or sacramental. The latter is a Bible-based sign in which individuals are given a welcome home to God and his church through the minister. This ministry complements the assurance of forgiveness that is given to all Christians through prayer and the promises of scripture. Why go to a minister and not directly to God? It's not either–or. When the lost son in Jesus' parable felt sorrow for his sins, he said, 'I will get up and go to my father, and I will say to him, "Father, I have sinned against heaven and before you"' (Luke 15:18). Imagine his coming home to a note on the table saying 'All is forgiven' rather than to a loving embrace. Sacramental confession helps many Christians to get that embrace and to know that when God says they are forgiven, *they are forgiven.* It can be helpful to confess specific sins to the pastor and to receive a welcome that signifies God's welcome to you as an individual.

It's significant that it was Easter Day when Christ gave authority for his disciples to pronounce absolution. From that day, the risen Christ, though invisible, has made himself present through signs— water, bread and wine, oil, touch—that we call sacraments. While the sacraments of baptism and Eucharist have Christ's clear authority, the other sacraments are valued in the church, including the ministry of forgiveness. Many find in such signs the healing touch of Jesus.

Going to sacramental confession is a challenge to name our sins before God so that we can be helped to overcome them. Around the time when I came back from my retreat with the God-sent demanding nun, I decided to start a prayer journal. I enter something in it day by day, following on from my formal time of prayer. It helps me look back not just over my prayer but over my life and spiritual milestones along the way. In it I talk to God as a discipline, about what I see as important and about my hopes and fears. Just as chatting to my wife, a friend or a spiritual director helps me see myself more fully—frail yet loved by God—so reading back what I have written in my journal gives me a more powerful sense of the spiritual journey I'm on, with God as my helper.

Besides scripture, spiritual books on the Christian life, such as this one, have value. When I find a helpful passage I copy it into my journal as a reminder. I can then look back at these passages on retreat days, taken on occasion at a local retreat house—a practice which I also commend for you. In last week's journal, for example, I wrote out this section of a spiritual book I've been reading:

> Of thy grace, O Lord, set a watch before my mouth and keep the door of my lips. Restrain me, save me from all dominance or display in conversation, from self-congratulation, open or disguised, from self-pleasing in play of words or wit, and all exaggeration for effect; from gossip, complaining and self-pity, from spite, hate and the will to wound, from discourtesy, harshness, cynicism and contempt, from worldly talk and laughter out of season. For I am utterly purposed that my mouth shall not offend. Rather, Lord, lead me to establish the disciplines of kindly speech, and sympathy of listening; the spirit of holy silence inwardly recollecting thee; and the joy of making melody in my heart with hymns and psalms and spiritual songs... *NON CLAMOR SED AMOR* [not talk but love].[41]

A passage like this can help us examine our sins of speech. Although we often need to put our personal situation on hold while we pray—to avoid selfish distraction away from the Lord—it is appropriate on occasion to make our own situation the starting point for prayer. Prayer is a bringing of the whole self to God—the negative (sins, fears, sickness, doubt, indiscretion) and the positive (gifts, relationships, church membership, and so on). Sometimes our daily prayer time can be a time of beseeching: 'Lord, show me my needs to be filled, my strengths to be consecrated.'

I reproduce below a suggested method of self-examination from my book *Meet Jesus*.

1 First, consciously enter the Lord's presence and cast your mind back over the last week, giving thanks for all the gifts you have received. Some may be great things and some seemingly insignificant—but all are gifts especially for you.
2 Notice, as you think back over the days, how the Lord has been working in you. What has he been asking of you? What has he been showing you?
3 What have your moods been during the week? Notice what brought you closer to the Lord. What has been his call to you? How did you respond?
4 Staying with your feelings, is there something that the Lord is showing you in a new way, something you would rather not look at, or something that the Lord is gently calling you to change? How do you want to respond?
5 Take a few moments to talk to the Lord about what you have discovered in this time of prayer and about any actions you feel called to take as a result of the prayer.
6 Ask for guidance and help through the coming week.[42]

Hand in hand

Any such examination of consciousness based on where you feel you have been can be complemented by checking your faithfulness to any Christian rule of life that you are committed to. This book has provided a fivefold template:

- Sunday church attendance
- daily formal and free prayer times
- ongoing study of the Bible and the church's faith
- time spent serving others
- regular self-examination and occasions for confession and guidance

The Christian discipline of reflection is a reminder of love, being loved and loving, and of our failure to love—in which attitudes are key. This book has at its heart a reminder to stick at loving God through five attitudes commended by Jesus Christ, knowing that 'we love because he first loved us' (1 John 4:19). The Lord Jesus gives us this overarching rule: 'You shall love the Lord your God with all your heart, and with all your soul, and with all your mind… You shall love your neighbour as yourself' (Matthew 22:37, 39). Loving God with our heart and soul can be seen as the purpose of worship and prayer, linked to loving him with our mind in study, our neighbour in service and ourself through reflection.

To experience Christ's love, we are therefore invited to follow five disciplines that are interrelated, like the thumb and fingers of the human hand, set to grasp the hand of God that reaches down to us in Jesus Christ. Worship and prayer are the heart and soul of our love for God, but Jesus implies that without engaging our minds with his teaching, our love will be ill formed. Without service (love of neighbour) and reflection (loving care of self), our love of God will be a delusion.

Like the *hamsa* hand symbol of hope and peace, the five loves invited by Jesus in Matthew 22:37–39 are a call to and reminder of balanced and effective discipleship. What's distinctive about Christian as opposed to other spiritual disciplines is the 'hand up' of grace that they engage with. If Christian disciplines attain salvation, they do so by grasping the hand of the Saviour. Experiencing Christ's love in the five disciplines of worship, prayer, study, service and reflection means taking God's hand in ours, welcoming his loving provision of forgiveness and healing that give us a hand up into his possibilities.

Worship, prayer, study, service and reflection are balanced disciplines. When two or three fail, we keep our grasp on God—or, rather, the Lord retains his grasp of us—through the disciplines that are still directed to him in the conduct of our lives. The chapters presented in this book remind us how important study and reflection actually are. Not only do they help to challenge the very many deceptions around us and within us, but through them our worship gains heart through understanding, our prayer gets kindled as God's word comes alive to us, and our service is made more effective by our better discernment of what God requires of us. In this way, in all our frailty we are brought to know the love of Christ, surpassing knowledge, with its downward (God to us), upward (us to God) and outward (God and us to the world) aspects.

Afterword

'All is grace.' The last words in *Diary of a Country Priest* sum up *Experiencing Christ's Love*. The God and Father of Jesus is a God of joyful goodness who loves us through and through and whose grace is overall and in all. That loving grace isn't a quantity so much as a quality of helpfulness given us by God, who simply desires it for us, not because we've done anything to earn it. This benevolence shown by God toward the human race is at the heart of the good news of Jesus.

> God, who is rich in mercy, out of the great love with which he loved us even when we were dead through our trespasses, made us alive together with Christ—by grace you have been saved— and raised us up with him and seated us with him in the heavenly places in Christ Jesus.
> **EPHESIANS 2:4-6**

To be raised up, we need to welcome and respond to God's grace, putting faith in him, placing our hand in his—and that means going out of our way. It's a countering of self-deception as expanded in this book. Attending worship may be inconvenient, but 'where there's a will, there's a way'. The discipline of prayer isn't necessarily accompanied by an awareness of God's presence. Awkward questions about the Bible matter, and there are times to get your head down to address them. We'll never be good at serving others without a readiness to shoulder life's little humiliations, which break the ego's shackle around us. Unless we are ready to examine ourselves regularly and confess our sins to God, 'the truth is not in us' (1 John 1:8).

Christians live under the favour of God, which is grace with a big aim— God's glory and the world's salvation—and a tight focus expressed as we worship on Sunday, pray every day, study the Bible, serve our neighbour and reflect upon our lives, confessing our sins. That big aim and tight focus are taken up into the love of Christ for God, for us and for all.

'All is grace.' The clue to effective living is to find that main thing, reaching out continually in worship, prayer, study, service and reflection to grasp 'the grace of the Lord Jesus Christ, the love of God, and the communion of the Holy Spirit' (2 Corinthians 13:13).

May you 'know the love of Christ that surpasses knowledge, so that you may be filled with all the fullness of God' (Ephesians 3:19).

Notes

1 Rudolf Otto, *The Idea of the Holy: An inquiry into the non-rational factor in the idea of the divine and its relation to the rational* (Oxford University Press, 1923).

2 Collect for the Twelfth Sunday after Trinity, *Common Worship: Services and Prayers for the Church of England* (The Archbishops' Council, 2000), p. 415.

3 Baron Friedrich von Hügel, *The Mystical Element of Religion* (Dent, 1923), p. 356.

4 Carey Nieuwhof, http://careynieuwhof.com/2015/02/10-reasons-even-committed-church-attenders-attending-less-often

5 Words from Holy Communion, *Book of Common Prayer* (1662).

6 John Twisleton, *Meet Jesus* (BRF, 2011), p. 63.

7 Rowan Williams, *Being Christian* (SPCK, 2014), p. 51.

8 George Guiver, *Everyday God* (Triangle, 1994), p. 77.

9 Minnie Louise Haskins, 'The Desert' (1912).

10 Twisleton, *Meet Jesus*, pp. 72–73.

11 John Twisleton, *Using the Jesus Prayer* (BRF, 2014), pp. 53–54.

12 Walter Hooper (ed.), *Daily Readings with C.S. Lewis* (Fount, 1992), p. 65.

13 See Joseph Tetlow (trans.), *The Spiritual Exercises of Ignatius of Loyola* (Crossroad, 2009).

14 Twisleton, *Using the Jesus Prayer*, pp. 9–10.

15 C.S. Lewis, *Miracles* (Fount, 1977 edn), pp. 134–135.

16 Carlo Rovelli, *Seven Brief Lessons on Physics*, trans. Simon Carnell and Erica Segre (Penguin, 2016).

17 Julius Purcell on Albert Camus, *The Tablet* (2 November 2013), pp. 15–16.

18 Apostles' Creed, *Common Worship*, p. 43.

19 Philip Schaff, *History of the Apostolic Church*, trans. Edward D. Yeoman (Scribner, Armstrong & Co, 1853), p. 568.

20 Richard Dawkins, *The God Delusion* (Bantam, 2006), p. 361.

21 Henri de Lubac, *The Religion of Teilhard de Chardin* (Collins, 1967), p. 230.

22 http://missionbibleclass.org/songs/songs-r/read-your-bible-pray-every-day-song

23 Collect for the Last Sunday after Trinity, *Common Worship*, p. 422.

24 *Bible Alive* monthly notes, Alive Publishing (www.alivepublishing.co.uk).

25 *Magnificat* monthly international booklet (www.magnificat.com).

26 *New Daylight*, BRF (www.biblereadingnotes.org.uk).

27 *WordLive* daily Bible study, Scripture Union (www.scriptureunion.org.uk).
28 *Word for Today* daily online Bible study, United Christian Broadcasters (www.ucb.co.uk).
29 E. Kadloubovsky and G.E.H. Palmer (trans.), *Writings from the Philokalia on Prayer of the Heart* (Faber & Faber, 1977).
30 Simon Tugwell, *Did You Receive the Spirit?* (DLT, 1972).
31 Kilian McDonnell and George T. Montague, *Christian Initiation and Baptism in the Holy Spirit* (Liturgical Press, 1991).
32 Richard Rohr interviewed by Jonathan Langley, *Christianity* (April 2016), p. 38.
33 'Grace by pain' in Eric Milner-White, *My God, My Glory* (SPCK, 1961), p. 163.
34 Cardinal Vincent Nichols, *A Pilgrimage Companion for the Year of Mercy* (Alive, 2015), pp. 42–53.
35 Pope Francis, *Amoris Laetitiae: The Joy of Love* (Catholic Truth Society, 2016), p. 149.
36 'And now, O Father, mindful of the love' (William Bright, 1824–1901).
37 Anglican-Roman Catholic International Commission, *The Final Report* (CTS/SPCK, 1982), p. 14.
38 Rovelli, *Seven Brief Lessons*, p. 1.
39 'What is this life if, full of care, we have no time to stand and stare?' from 'Leisure' in W.H. Davies, *Collected Poems* (Knopf, 1916), p. 18.
40 Oliver Cromwell in a letter to the general assembly of the Church of Scotland, 1650 (www.olivercromwell.org/quotes1.htm).
41 'Grace of speech and silence' in Milner-White, *My God, My Glory*, p. 160.
42 Twisleton, *Meet Jesus*, p. 90.

Acknowledgements

We do not grasp the love of God in Christ on our own but 'with all the saints' (Ephesians 3:18). I'm grateful to the apostle Paul and other biblical writers for helping me find that grasp, so vividly spoken of in the letter to the Ephesians.

I acknowledge the service of my parents, Elsie and Greg, and my grandmother Eliza in my growth towards God, supplemented by my housemaster, John Dean, and Giggleswick School chaplain, Philip Curtis, who prepared me for confirmation. My chemical research supervisor, John White, and St John's College chaplain Eric Heaton played a formative role in getting me thinking about God. Fr John Hooper, former vicar of St Mary Magdalene, Oxford, did much in my student years to serve my discovery of Christ's love in the sacraments and the value of spiritual direction. Canon Eric Ashby, Bishop Graham Leonard, Canon Charles Smith and John Teasdale, several monks of the Community of the Resurrection and Community of the Servants of the Will of God, priest brothers of the Company of Mission Priests and Society of the Holy Cross (SSC) have helped me experience the church, with all its shortfalls, as 'the fullness of [Jesus] who fills all in all' (Ephesians 1:23).

I am grateful to the writers Hans Urs von Balthasar, Teilhard de Chardin, Austin Farrer, Thomas Merton, Eric Milner-White, Henri Nouwen, Michael Ramsey, Saint Thérèse of Lisieux, Colin Urquhart, Robert Warren, David Watson and the authors of the Orthodox *Philokalia* for their inspiration, as well as the Cursillo, New Wine and Vassula Ryden's True Life in God networks and my associates at Premier Christian Radio.

I acknowledge the way my wife, Anne, continues to inspire me by her own deep experience of Christ's love.

Finally, I thank the many friends and church members I have learned from over the years, in England and Guyana, along with Karoline Peach for her suggestions on the book as it evolved, and my commissioning editor Mike Parsons and the staff of The Bible Reading Fellowship.

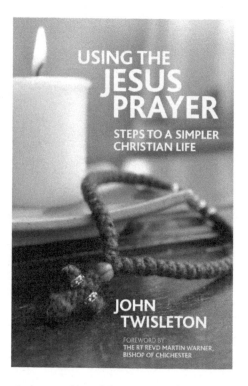

For over 15 centuries repetition of the prayer 'Lord Jesus Christ, Son of God, have mercy on me, a sinner' has been an effective and practical way to cool the mind of anxiety and stress, and enrich the spirit. Drawing on his own faith journey and pastoral experience, John Twisleton describes how he was called to welcome the Jesus Prayer as a surprising gift of the Holy Spirit. He shares how use of the prayer brings a gift of simplicity that counters the postmodern fragmentation of Christian life, as individuals and groups seek truth away from what is traditional and institutional teaching.

Using the Jesus Prayer
Steps to a simpler Christian life
John Twisleton

978 0 84101 778 5 £6.99

brfonline.org.uk

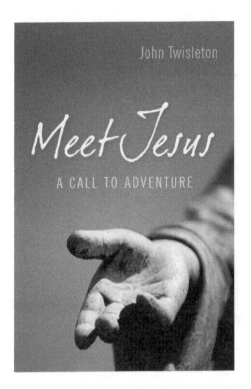

To engage with Jesus expands the mind and heart. It challenges our view of the way the world is, where it is heading and what difference we could make to it. But in a world of competing philosophies, where does Jesus fit in? How far can we trust the Bible and the Church? What difference does Jesus make to our lives and our communities? Is Jesus really the be all and end all? *Meet Jesus* is a lively and straightforward exploration of these and other questions, with the aim of engaging our reason, inspiring our faith and worship, deepening our fellowship and service, and bringing new depth to our witness to the world.

Meet Jesus
A call to adventure
John Twisleton
978 0 84101 895 9 £7.99

brfonline.org.uk

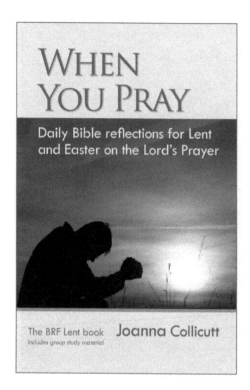

In these Bible readings for Lent and Easter, Joanna Collicutt shows how growing as a Christian is rooted in the prayer Jesus gave us. As we pray the Lord's Prayer, we express our relationship with God, absorb gospel values and are also motivated to live them out. As we pray to the Father, in union with the Son, through the power of the Spirit, so we begin to take on the character of Christ.

When You Pray
Daily Bible reflections for Lent and Easter
on the Lord's Prayer
Joanna Collicutt
978 0 85746 089 9 £7.99

brfonline.org.uk

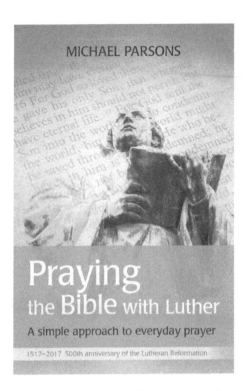

MICHAEL PARSONS

Praying
the Bible with Luther

A simple approach to everyday prayer

1517–2017 500th anniversary of the Lutheran Reformation

Beginning each time of prayer with a Bible passage, Luther would meditate on it with four 'strands' in mind: teaching, thanksgiving, repentance and supplication. Then he would pray, having his thoughts shaped by his reading, praying God's words after him, confident of God's grace. *Praying the Bible with Luther* explains this method, demonstrates it and encourages readers to follow his example, helping us to turn scripture into prayer and to pray it into our own lives today.

Praying the Bible with Luther
A simple approach to everyday prayer
Michael Parsons
978 0 85746 503 0 £8.99

brfonline.org.uk